Song *of My* *People*

LIAM LAWTON

VERITAS

Published 2002 by
Veritas Publications
7/8 Lower Abbey Street
Dublin I
Ireland

Email: publications@veritas.ie
Website: www.veritas.ie

ISBN I 85390 600 X

A catalogue for this book is available from the British Library.

Veritas books are printed on paper made from the wood pulp of managed forests. For every tree felled, at least one tree is planted, thereby renewing natural resources.

Cover design by Pierce Design
Printed by Betaprint Ltd

Song of
my People

Also by Liam Lawton

Molaise
Light the Fire
The Clouds' Veil
Ancient Ways Future Days
Sacred Story
The Shepherd Boy
Journey Of A Soul
In The Quiet

In Caelo (editor)

For my grandparents
William and Anne Lawton, Frank and Brigid Cunningham
& my grand-aunt Mary-Joe Carey

⨯ Contents

Suantraí ∾ *Songs of Dreams*

Acknowledgements

Over the past number of years, through my work and music, I have become aware of the richness of my roots, the tradition and spirituality that I was born in to. It has always been my wish to share such wealth, hence the writing of this book – a series of reflections on the people, customs and wisdom that have influenced my music and composition over the past 10 years.

I owe much gratitude to those who made this possible. To Maura Hyland and Maureen Saunders at Veritas for their support and encouragement, to Toner Quinn for editing.

To Michael Cymbala and Sarah Parker and all at GIA Publications, Chicago, for their help and continued support. To my colleagues and friends who perform and enhance my music by their presence.

To Marian Gaynor, John McCann and John Drummond who have played an important role in shaping my music over the years.

To Helen Whelan whose help and assistance is invaluable. To my parents, family and friends, and to all those mentioned between the covers of this book who through their wisdom, inspiration and lives have taught me to sing proudly… the song of my people.

Prologue

Nestling in the rolling foothills of east Cork is the townsland of Kilcredan. If you climb the hills you look out towards Ballycotton Bay whose lighthouse has saved many a sailor over the centuries as they make their journey towards Cobh and Cork harbour. To the east is the village of Ballymacoda, home of the great Irish poet Piaras Mac Gearailt. Now a *Breac-Gaeltacht* (Irish is now not the spoken language), it once was the home of a great Irish tradition in language and music, with many a song echoing from the calm waters of Knockadoon.

It was from Kilcredan that my grandfather William gathered his belongings on a Spring morning in 1910 and headed westwards to Queenstown, or Cobh as it was later known. Like so many of his generation and those before him, he was going to seek his fortune in far off 'Amerikay'. The country was still suffering the remnants of the Great Famine and many could remember stories of the poisoned earth and the bitter mourning. So many had sailed from the same pier, so many had never returned.

William, my grandfather, was typical of a lad of his age – a burning ambition to better himself and to seek a better life. He carried with him his meagre possessions, but sacred to him was his concertina, music to gladden the heart in lonelier times.

The passengers would board a small tender which would then take them to the waiting ship, some distance beyond the shoreline. The pier was the place of tears and promises – only the brave could dare to look back. In silent numbness they entered the boat to the background of pitiful moans and cries. Slowly and quietly on this day my grandfather picked up the concertina and played the air of the old Fenian anthem – 'God Save Ireland'. Those alongside him began to hum and then sing the song, while soon the tune was picked up by those standing on the pier. Soon the daylight was broken by the sound of song as those left behind sang their loved ones into a new world. Those who left the shore left with the memory of song and the notes of a concertina falling one after another in an inexpressible language that quietens the heart when all else fails. United in song and sorrow, my grandfather's passion would pass to the generations yet unborn.

Though my grandfather had sung himself into the 'new world', he was soon to sing himself back into the 'old world' as after two years he found himself back in east Cork having inherited a farm holding. Soon he was to settle down and marry Anne O'Callaghan from Churchland, Ballymacoda. She was a well-known traditional singer and performed at many a wedding and wake in the locality. By the time of her death in 1961, she had amassed a great store of songs. They reared eleven children, my father being the youngest, and instilled in their offspring a love of all things Irish which my father still carries today.

In time, my father left the sheltering beauty of the east Cork landscape and found his way to the boglands of east Offaly, working as an Inspector in the Department of Agriculture. In Offaly he settled in the town of Edenderry but married a young girl from Tullamore. By fate, my mother's family – Cunninghams – were themselves steeped in a musical heritage and were the founder members of the Offaly branch of Comhaltas Ceoltoirí Éireann, an organisation that promotes the protection and development of Irish traditional music. The Cunningham Brothers showband found its way into many a dance hall in the 1950s in the midlands of Ireland playing the hits of the day, but never far behind was a treasure trove of Irish tunes, sessions and songs.

It was from this union of the east Cork Gaeltacht and a midlands town that my twin brother Tom and I were born, followed later by my brothers Gay, John and my sister Marie. Never far from our door was the sound of song in all styles and forms. Piano was taught to us by an elderly nun who had greater sympathies with Chopin than with O'Carolan – but it was these lessons that formed the basis of my knowledge today. As a young boy I often recall sitting on my grandfather's knee in Tullamore as he played the 'Rakes of Mallow' and other such tunes on his Walton's Whistle. My grandaunt Mary-Joe had a wealth of Irish songs, and her home in Kilbeggan was the place of many great Irish sessions. Though a small little woman, her heart was as big as many of the great Irish heroes she sang about.

It was as a young secondary school student that I first came in contact with the music of Seán Ó Riada. In the summer, we would head back to east Cork to the town of Castlemartyr, which was the home of Coláiste Ultáin where my father himself had been educated. It was during these days that I was exposed to the sounds and songs of the Horslips, Clannad, Planxty and the Bothy Band. Another favourite was the Breton harpist, Alan Stivell. I can still remember the songs that kissed my soul. Like any other teenager at the time, I immersed myself in the music of the day, but the real well-spring that I returned to was the music of tradition. Like rich honey that ferments over time, so too did the ancient music of this ancient land – the song of my people.

This prepared the way for me to begin my studies at the National University of Maynooth, where I began to read Irish Studies and English Literature. After completing my second year I decided that I wanted to enter the seminary and study theology, so when my B.A. was complete, I did so. It was here that I experienced the beauty of Gregorian chant. Dr Sean Lavery was the Director of Music at the seminary and for a number of years I sang with the College Chapel Choir. Whenever I revisit the beautiful Gunn Chapel I am haunted by the sounds and songs of those years. In July 1984 I was ordained for the diocese of Kildare and Leighlin and appointed to Carlow Cathedral. After seven years, I returned to my Alma Mater at Maynooth to study for the Higher Diploma in Education and was subsequently appointed to the staff of Knockbeg College, Carlow, where I served for seven more years. During this time the creative process was fermenting within, and eventually in 1990 I decided to explore the possibility of composing new Irish liturgical music. The voice of Máire Brennan and Clannad had continued to haunt me since the years when I was a young student, and therein I found a vehicle to present a new image of sacred music – music that stirred the soul.

My first collection, *Molaise*, was followed by six others, and as I write these pages I am about to return to the US to record a new collection. What unfolds in these pages is the stories behind these songs, their birthing and their finding a home in Irish life and beyond. No song is without a story and no story is without its own struggle and blessing.

The vehicle that I have used to put these songs into context is borrowed from the ancient Celtic tradition that divides music into three types – *geantraí*, *goltraí* and *suantraí*. I hope such stories will open a window into a beautiful and rich culture that continues to enthral me as I delve into its ancient history. May all who journey through these pages find some moment to quieten the heart; listen and be still and hear on the wind – the song of my people.

Liam Lawton, December 2001

Geantraí, Goltraí & Suantraí

It is said that, in ancient times, Irish music was divided into three types. According to ancient literature, it referred mainly to instrumental music. However, I will be broadening this canvas in the pages ahead. The terms *geantraí*, *goltraí* and *suantraí* refer to the music of joy and laughter, the music of tears, and the music of sleeping.

Legend has it that Geantraí, Goltraí and Suantraí were three brothers. Their father was Uaithne, a harpist, and their mother was Boand, a goddess. When she was in labour, Uaithne played on his harp. It was crying and moaning with her in the intensity of her pains at the beginning; it was laughing and joyful with her in the middle of them at the pleasure of having brought forth two sons; and it was repose and tranquility with her on the birth of the last son after the weight of labour. It was because of this that each of them was named after a type of music. Boand then awoke from repose. 'Accept thou thy three sons, O passionate Uaithne,' said she, 'in return for thy generosity, namely laughing music, crying music and sleeping music.'

Elsewhere the names are derived from the music played on a harp that has but three strings. A brass string that was known as *geantairghléas*, which when played brought great laughter; a silver string called *goltairghléas* which when played brought tears and sorrow; and finally an iron string named *suantairghléas* which when played caused a deep slumber.

For over a thousand years such was the literary convention to explain the origin of music in Ireland, but for me it is a noble way to define music written for a new generation in an ancient land.

Geantraí

Songs of Joy & Laughter

'This day was made by the Lord
we rejoice and are glad' (Ps. 118)

Molaise

*M*y story as a liturgical composer begins in the spring of 1990. At the time
I was at the Cathedral of the Assumption, Carlow, and I prepared a work
for a liturgical service during an Arts Festival known as 'Éigse Ceatharlach'.
Éigse is the ancient Celtic term for a group of poets who came together to
perform their work. The music I had prepared was entitled 'Molaise'.

Being influenced by the music of the past as well as the music of
contemporary composers, I had a great desire to write a new Mass setting in
the Irish language that would incorporate both traditional and contemporary
musical instruments and sounds. It was in the beginning of the revival of all
things Celtic and I believed that it was also time for the church that I belonged
to to explore new ways of celebrating our faith. Peadar Ó Riada, son of the late
great Seán Ó Riada, one of Ireland's finest composers, had once said to me, 'to
maintain a proper sense of balance, we must be like a three-legged stool, and
thus have a leg in the past, a leg in the present and a leg in the future'. I couldn't
argue!

Where does one search for inspiration when writing sacred or secular
music? Such a journey will always take us on an internal as well as an external
journey to the places that offer life. On such an occasion I could look no
further than he who brought the message of Christianity to the place that is
now my home. This is the story of the one they called Lazerian.

Away in the hills of Carlow was the village of the 'half-glen' called Leighlin.
Tradition has it that on his arrival at Leighlin on the banks of the River Barrow,
St Patrick and his disciples saw a host of angels hovering nearby. Asked what
the vision signified, Patrick said, 'Some years from now a faithful servant of
God named Lazerian will dwell here and the number of his disciples shall be as
great as that host of angels.'

Born around 566 of noble Ulster descent, Lazerian was noted for his piety.
He spent his childhood at the court of King Aidan in Scotland, who was the
father of his mother Gemma. Returning to Ireland he was placed under the care

of a certain monk named Munnu and returned to live on a remote Scottish island as a hermit. From there he sailed for Rome to study theology, was ordained by Pope Gregory the Great, and commissioned to preach the gospel in Ireland. With his disciples he travelled the country preaching until, after some thought, he decided to settle in the area now known as Leighlin. The village was soon to become a great centre of learning visited by many from far and near.

Around this time there was a discrepancy between the Celtic and the Roman method of calculating when Easter should be celebrated. In 630 Lazerian went to Rome to discuss the matter with the Pope. With their meagre means of transport, the journey was a hazardous one. In 630 the Universal Church celebrated the feast of Easter on the 21st of April. The pope was Pope Monarious. In 633 he consecrated Lazerian as bishop and appointed him a legate in Ireland. Lazerian convened a synod of bishops in Ireland and eventually the new date of Easter was accepted. The area of Leighlin was the first place in Ireland to adopt the new date.

Lazerian was now bishop and the monastery at Old Leighlin was flourishing. It is said that at one stage over 1500 monks inhabited it. In the history written about the life of a certain St Magnean of Kilmainham it is said that once, while on a visit to Lazerian, he came and found him lying in a hovel with many diseases. Lazerian said: 'I declare it Holy Bishop, my condition is revealed to me, my sinfulness goes thro' my body and I want to have my purgatory here and eternal life on the other side. As the grain of wheat must be threshed and beaten before it is sown in the earth, so with me before I am laid in the grave. I would have my body threshed with infirmities.' Lazerian then asked Magnean to preside at his funeral. He was buried under the High Cross in the foothills of Leighlin. His monastery was to become an orphanage, a great centre of prayer and Christian education.

This piece of instrumental music was also the title of my very first recorded collection. It was recorded at the Glór na nGael studios in Dublin and through the support of a great *Gaeilgeoir* (Irish speaker) in Carlow – Bríd de Róiste – I succeeded in recording my first ever collection. Using the choir of the Cathedral of the Assumption and some fine soloists, I gathered a group of Irish musicians around me that were to become my comrades in the years ahead. Little did I think while recording on a wet murky weekend in Dublin how my life would change as I began to sing the ancient songs of my people.

Some months later I gave the first performance of this work at a music summer school. I was extremely nervous but all went well until I became aware of an elderly gentleman in the audience who was weeping. Of all the people present at the recital that evening my attention became fixed on him, so worried was I that my composition had upset him. When the performance was concluded I saw him coming towards me and I feared the worst. As I prepared to apologise to him he put out his hand and said, 'I am so sorry but I haven't cried in years. Whatever affect the music had on me it allowed me the space for tears. It has touched something deep inside me.'

As I write these lines I still remember the night vividly, when I dared to show something of my own to the world for the very first time, when the crowd cheered, and an old man cried.

Molaigí an Tiarna
Molaigí an Rí
Molaigí ár Slánitheoir
Molaigí an Chríost

Canaigí go glórmhor
Canaigí go h-ard
Canaigí go croíúil
Canaigí le grá.

GATHER
And we'll Gather and we shall reap
And no longer in sadness we'll weep
And we'll Gather and we shall reap
Resting, Rising, Calling, Guiding
O Lord

LIGHT THE FIRE

Gather

Language is full of memory and within our Celtic tradition is a store of poetic wealth. The Gaelic (Irish) language can express an abundance of thoughts and words in a single phrase. Much of our language is imbued with spiritual undertones that when translated can often lose its beauty and depth of richness.

One word within the Irish tradition that I particularly like is the word *muintearas*. Its onomatopoeic sound resonates with music and yet it is so difficult to translate properly.

Muintir in the Irish language means 'people', but *muintearas* is akin to 'peopleness' – but is there such a word? At the heart of Irish life was the notion of community, and *muintearas* refers to the sense of community that exists between people. It is about belonging. There is a deep need within all of us to belong. It is more than attachment to people over things. It is a hunger within the human condition, within the human soul.

Christianity is the language of community. It is a communal religion and finds its meaning in service to and with others. The high point of the Christian week is the communal gathering on the Lord's Day, when work is put aside and the community gathers to give thanks to God and to support and bless one another.

The Christian notion of community sees it as a place of healing, a place of resting and a place of promise. The piece 'Gather' is a communal song full of invitation in which I use the ancient Irish image of the crossroads. So many experiences happened at the crossroads – they were the place of meeting, the place of music and song, the place of departure and the place of decision. They were also the places that led people home. So many emotions and memories are tied up with these places. 'Gather' is about invitation – to invite all with no prejudices – to gather to celebrate the presence of God in the community, a place where *all* people are welcome. Not a select few.

On further reflection, however, we discover that our communities are not often a place of welcome, but with increased urbanisation has come increased isolation. The key in the latch is replaced by countless alarms and locks, hospitality by hostility. The refugee and asylum seeker may knock on many a door before there is a welcome.

This piece, 'Gather', is from my first English language collection *Light The Fire*. It appeared in 1996. When I think back to this time of my life, I realise that I too was at a crossroads. I had just finished in pastoral ministry at our Cathedral and had begun a teaching post at Knockbeg College, our diocesan college. There I began to explore the possibilities of composing new liturgical music.

Lack of direction, funding and proper structures can often hinder such designs, however, and I suffered in this regard. But I was also fired by a great desire to write new music and was ready to face any obstacle – and there were many! It can be so difficult for someone unknown to make inroads into what might be perceived as an already established business.

Through a series of events I was led in the direction of some good souls who were prepared to back me financially and offer me a contract. The collection *Light The Fire* had its birth in a small studio. Each week I would gather with a group of friends – musicians and singers – to record and rehearse and record. Many times when I lost hope and belief in the project, Paul the engineer and his wife Maureen continued to offer support and encouragement. They created their own sense of community with their hospitality and welcome. Slowly and surely the collection took shape as my weekends and those of my friends were sacrificed to complete our goal. It had taken me almost two years to write and record. However, such times and trials are forgotten when someone is touched or uplifted by the music. Then it all makes sense.

Recently a friend of mine helped a fellow student to move house in the United States. As he shifted some of her belongings a cassette fell to the floor. The girl who was moving house was from Singapore and the cassette that fell was *Light The Fire*. Surprised and shocked my friend asked her, 'Where did you get this?', to which she replied, 'In Singapore, I listen to it all the time.'

And the beauty of this story is that: no it wasn't a boot-legged copy but an original one — composed in Carlow, recorded in Maynooth, sold in Dublin, bought in...?

And we'll gather and we shall reap
And no longer in sadness we'll weep
And we'll gather and we shall weep
Resting, Rising, Calling Guiding
O Lord.

HOLY IS GOD
Now share the story, now we recall
How God leads the children who answer the call.
Now remember all those in need
God comes to comfort the hungry to feed

CLOUDS' VEIL

Holy Is God

The oral tradition of telling stories, reciting poems and singing songs found a great home in Ireland. From the time of the Celts, whose culture remained unconquered by the Romans, thus allowing the rich Celtic mythology to survive, stories have been told and retold.

In rural communities in Ireland up to the twentieth century the 'seanachie' or storyteller had a special place in the hearts of these communities. The seanachie had the power to allow the natural to become the supernatural, the power to transform bleak and powerless lives into worlds full of dreams and fantasy. It is said that at times of storytelling all Irish people are children – from eight to eighty. No matter how often a story has been told, something new will always emerge.

It was the seanachie – the storyteller – who helped to keep communities together by keeping alive the spirit of its people. Each locality had its own history, its own characters, its own life.

Very often the stories told throughout the country shared similar characteristics or motifs: the notion of hospitality was central, as when a stranger called, or stories that dealt with the thin veil between this world and the 'other world', or the gender struggles between men and women for power and authority, or the presence of the Divine in the ordinariness of everyday life, and the power of nature.

At times passionate, satirical or even sentimental, the storyteller verbalised the life and soul of a particular community. These were the stories that were carried in hearts and minds across borders and oceans, skies and seas. Ireland was never far from the pain of exile and emigration and the stories were told and retold in far off lands. For those in far away places, the place of birth and home becomes immortalised in wild imagination. As one writer in the last century wrote, 'The Irish tale, no less than the Irish poem, has grown as the rose in the night, scattering its fragrance on the four winds and leading the lovers of freshness, tint and perfection to a satisfaction afforded by no other garden of the world. The Irish have even rocked the cradle of the fanciful and stood sponsors to the natural touch of fiction. Thatched roofs and smoke-stained rooms have even been those of castles wherein rainbowed spirits, whom the heaviest heel of oppression could not crush, have plucked the chords of "Inspiration's Lyre".'

In the Christian tradition and in the Jewish tradition, passing on the 'story' from one generation to the next was equally important. Jesus told stories throughout his ministry and then these stories or parables are told and retold through the centuries to this present day. For those of us who belong to the Christian tradition the challenge is to relate the stories of Jesus so they can give meaning to our very busy and, at times, noisy lives.

'Holy is God' is what I term a gathering song – it is an invitation to gather and remember the story of Jesus, but also an opportunity for the community to gather and share its own story – the struggles, joys and blessings of its people.

When I am in Carlow I celebrate the Eucharist on a Sunday in a retirement home called St Fiach's House. It is a special place and I always receive a great welcome and the best of Irish hospitality. I am often struck by the wisdom of those who have 'lived life' and seen other days. Too often we can become so absorbed in our own story that we don't have time to listen to the stories of others.

Often we need people to hear our story, to take time and listen. Sadly there are those who are never heard and have no one to listen, all they have are memories of what could have been. If we don't have time to listen to others, it is highly unlikely that we will find the time to listen to what is going on within ourselves.

When I recorded the song 'Holy Is God' it was in new and unfamiliar surroundings. It was in the city of Minneapolis, in the home of the well-known liturgical composer Marty Haugen, and engineered by Gary Daigle, two people who have given much to the life of my music. Here in Minnesota I had to learn to listen to other creative voices, people with experience and wisdom but who also ensured that my contribution was heard.

For two weeks we spent many hours in the studio, recording, tracking and rehearsing. It was my first experience of recording outside of Ireland and I slowly became aware of how others could shape and influence my own direction, that I didn't have all the answers myself. In the midst of gracious hospitality it slowly dawned on me that when I sit and listen to the song of my neighbour I am never as poor again and am all the more blessed because they see the world very differently than I do. These early days of recording were to open many doors for me later in the USA.

Holy, holy is God
God of all wisdom, God of the word
Holy, holy is God
God ever faithful, God of all love.

HOW CAN I REPAY
How can I repay the Lord
for his goodness to me.

LIGHT THE FIRE

How Can I Repay The Lord

*T*he Irish people have never been known to be slow to celebrate. From as far back as we can ascertain there have always been reasons or occasions for celebration. In the Celtic world many celebrations were built around the ancient calendar of events or great feasts. The four great feasts of the year were *Samhain* (1st November), *Imbolg* (1st February), *Bealtaine* (1st May) and *Lughnasa* (1st August). Notice that each of the feasts begins each of the four seasons of the year – winter, spring, summer and autumn.

These feasts were influenced by the solstices and the equinoxes. The different feast days gave the people their various reasons to celebrate. One of the great times of celebration was the ancient feast of *Samhain* – Halloween. At *Samhain* the herds of cattle and sheep were led down the mountains to shelter. It was a time for the community to take stock. It is a threshold time – the summer is now over and the winter is about to begin. It was traditionally the beginning of the Celtic year. It is the period between chaos and order. The 'other world' and this world become intertwined and people moved between one and the other. In many parts of Ireland people dress up on the feast of *Samhain*. The disguise allows for ease of movement between the two worlds as it becomes impossible to distinguish who is who. Gates are symbolically removed and doors left unopened to allow easy access from one world to another.

As a young boy, I remember going from house to house singing and performing, hoping to acquire some reward and getting up to all kinds of devilment. I didn't realise then the significance of this 'threshold time', when two worlds are intertwined and time is suspended. In the Christian calendar, the 'Feast of All Saints' is celebrated on this day and this is followed the next day by the 'Feast of All Souls'. A widespread belief was that the dead members and relatives of the family returned to their old home for this particular night. Hospitality was essential to help the travellers on their journey. Fires were lit and neighbours gathered to recall the great heroes of the past.

Such nights were the cause of great celebration and merry making. Today many places still gather to celebrate the foundations of their Christian heritage within their local area. Patterns, field days and festivals have continued through the centuries and provide an opportunity for a community to come together. In Ireland such celebrations were essential to the fabric of rural life.

'How Can I Repay The Lord' recalls the many blessings that we experience in our lives through people, places and experiences. Through music I have received many blessings in my own life which have become sources of much inspiration.

A few years ago I found myself in the far north of the Scottish Highlands in a rugged but beautiful place called Forth William. In a castle owned by the McFarlane-Barrow clan, I took part in a great evening of traditional music and song from Ireland and Scotland. The son of the owner of the establishment was a renowned Scottish fiddler and I was entranced by the beauty of the music of the Scottish Islands, the Hebrides.

While people lived in great poverty on these islands in the past, the cultural life was highly developed with no shortage of musicians, storytellers and singers. Like our own tradition people would gather in neighbouring houses to share song and story. It was here, according to Irish scholar Seán Ó Duinn, that the *ceilí* was developed – where people gathered nightly for traditional entertainment. The stories of past heroes were recalled and the poems and songs of past generations were handed down to another time.

One of the greatest folklorists of the Celtic tradition was Alexander Carmichael whose work covers six volumes and has been translated from Scots Gaelic into English. His work, known as the *Carmina Gadelica*, was collected between 1855 and 1899. This collection has become one of the greatest sources of inspiration for me and I find myself constantly returning to it when writing. It is a collection of prayers, hymns, incantations, blessings, rites and ancient tradition of all kinds, giving a beautiful insight into the lives of these people. It recalls the nights of songs and stars, of boats and blessings, of child and creation:

The old people conversed about the state of the world and about changes in the weather, about the moon and the sun, about the stars of the sky, about the ebbing and flowing of the sea, about the life in the depths of the ocean, and about the hot and cold lands of the earth (Carmina Gadelica 3, 21).

That night in Fortwilliam we played music and sang into the late hours of morning as the moon cast its shadow over the lakes of the Scottish Highlands. Never far was the belief that God was only a breath away and would never separate Himself for too long from these people. In true Scottish tradition the fire was 'smoored' (quenched but not fully) before we said goodnight and the ancient blessing was prayed...

I smoor this night my fire
as Mary's son would smoor
God's compassing be to myself and the fire
God's compassing to myself and to all
God's compassing to myself and the hearth
God's compassing to myself and the floor
and upon each herd and flock
and upon the household all.

SONG FOR ÓRAN
Glory to God in the Highest
And peace to God's people
God's people on earth

LIGHT THE FIRE

Song For Óran

I have always been made curious by how other people view the world and particularly how those of past days saw the world around them. It is sometimes too easy to consign traditional belief to the ignorance of the past. Very often the wisdom of age is passed over for the sake of progress and modernity. I am quite certain that the quest to understand the meaning of the Divine in life today is very much similar to the questions asked by our forebearers. Yes, life may have been less complicated, but there was always questions – a searching for God.

Within an island culture, traditions have always been slower to change as there is, in a sense, protection, being surrounded by the security of the sea. Thus there was always great rejoicing when the island was blessed with a new birth. The life and future was ensured with the continuation of a family line.

One beautiful island tradition that I came across concerns the process of birth. It seems that of all the people revered and respected within the island culture the midwife was held in particular high regard. She was the one blest to protect and guide the new life into the world. When she was present, women felt secure. In some descriptions they speak of the 'kind matronly woman without fear, who coaxed and cajoled the new offspring to brave their way into the waiting world'.

It was said that the midwife prayed constantly that the awaited child would be born at the time of the incoming tide. When the child was duly born, it was the midwife who took the child down to the seashore and taking three droplets of water blessed the new-born in the name of God the Father, God the Son and

God the Holy Spirit. Then holding the child up, she prayed that all sickness, all evil and all harm would be washed away on the outgoing tide. What a beautiful image.

The Gloria is found in the Gospel narrative of the four evangelists when writing of the birth of Jesus. It is the song of angels and has been written into our Eucharistic celebration as a song of praise and thanksgiving to the Creator God.

When writing the Gloria to music for the *Light The Fire* collection, my brother and his family eagerly awaited the birth of their second child. He was born six years to the day as I write this, a little boy called Óran. His name is an ancient Irish name, mentioned in our history as a young boy who was the charioteer of St Patrick. His birth brought great joy to our lives, but like all children he, his brothers and sisters, and all children, are but a reflection of the beauty of the dream of God. Like the midwife of old who blessed the young born with the sacred waters of the tide, we should not lose our tradition of blessing our children each day as they too make their journey on the tide of life.

For you alone are the holy one
You alone are the Lord
You alone are the most high Jesus Christ
With the Holy Spirit
In the glory of God the Father,
Amen.

THE HERMIT SONG
Take this song to share
Take this silent prayer
Take your rest in still of day
So shall you know
So shall you go
So shall you know
The quiet call

LIGHT THE FIRE

The Hermit Song

_H_ave you ever noticed how the early Irish monks chose beautiful but obscure places to build their first settlements in the early years of Christianity in this country? Many parishes in rural Ireland shelter the hidden remains of Christian settlements. Probably one of the most fascinating of all monastic settlements is Scellig Mhicil, the rock island off the wild and windswept Atlantic coast.

As monastic life flourished, so also did the desire to be at one with God. Places of quiet and solitude were highly sought, as the influence of the spirituality of the early desert fathers in Egypt began to find inroads in the Irish spiritual way of life. Through contemplation the eyes of saintly men and women were washed clean, enabling them to see the world with a much greater clarity.

In Glendalough, County Wicklow, we can visit the cave where St Kevin would ponder the mystery of God's presence. In wooded vales or isolated lakesides the ways of the world were renounced. Patrick climbed the mountain, the Reek in County Mayo, already a holy site in the pre-Christian world, to find solace and inspiration. In the Old Testament God calls his people into the wilderness to communicate with them, likewise the Irish monks seek out such places of contemplation. It is in the wilderness that obedience and discipline in

God's purpose and promise unfolded. The place of the desert lies at the heart of the Christian experience of God.

For me, there is something quite stark yet beautiful about the Celtic wilderness. Windswept, misty and green, it has afforded the hermit with many opportunities for quiet contemplation in sacred spaces and places. Fourteen years ago I first came across the Carthusian monastery of St Hugh's Charterhouse. Set in the rolling foothills of Horsham in South England, it was to become a place of comfort and consolation in my hectic and busy life.

What drew me there was the kind and earthy soul of Dom Bruno Sullivan. For almost sixty years, he has lived in silent contemplation of the mystery of God in the Carthusian way of life. To some it may seem austere, to others senseless, but I have never once believed that such a life is lived to escape from the trials of worldly life. To live a life of prayer and contemplation means that one must live with one's self twenty-four hours a day, seven days a week and so on, probably the most difficult feat for all of us.

As my relationship of trust with Dom Bruno grew through his constant letters and my subsequent visits, I began to experience a window into this quiet and beautiful world. I received many consolations and many challenges. As I put my head to rest each night I knew somewhere in the world men and women like Dom Bruno were beginning their night vigil for the world outside. As I celebrated Christmas Day with my family and friends, I was aware that these saintly men keep a day of vigil with the Lord while the rest of the world celebrates.

Last August Dom Bruno slipped quietly from this world into the world that he contemplated all his life. He never feared death and was at pains to speak always of a loving God. I miss him deeply. I wrote the song 'Hermit Song' for him and am grateful to God that before he left this world, with a small battery-operated cassette recorder in his quiet cell, he heard his song.

Swiftly bird flies in heaven's praise
Swift swirls the clouds in ocean's gaze
Swift flow my thoughts through endless days
That I might sing the song of praise

THE MASS OF THE CELTIC SAINTS

Kyrie eleison

Christe eleison

Kyrie eleison

CLOUDS' VEIL

The Mass of the Celtic Saints

*I*n Celtic spirituality there was always room for the stranger. They could easily be a visitor from the 'other world' or even Christ himself in the guise of the stranger. There are many beautiful poems and prayers from our tradition to welcome a guest in our midst.

> And I put food in the eating place
> drink in the drink place and
> music in the music place.

And so grew the tradition of hospitality where doors were always open and nobody was left hungry. To offer food and hospitality to the stranger was seen as a blessing, as one never knew when and how the blessing might return as reward.

In the summer of 1997 I was attending a Church music summer school at my Alma Mater, Maynooth College, when I was introduced to a visitor who had come from the United States. Sitting on a grey and wet miserable afternoon, I had no idea how such an encounter was to affect my life and music. My guest had recently been bereaved and belonged to a very close-knit circle of family and friends, all second and third generation Irish who had settled in Chicago. Mary Jule Durkin had come to commission an Irish artist to compose some sacred music in honour of her deceased husband Jack, but also music that would serve the Liturgy. And so it befell on myself to compose such music. It was through this encounter that I was to experience another facet of the Irish spirit, so alive and exciting in a far away land.

I decided to compose a Mass setting which I titled *The Mass of the Celtic Saints*. It would be sung at the parish of Old St Patrick's, situated in the heart of Chicago, at the north-west corner of Adams and Des Plaines streets. Old St Patrick's Church is the oldest public building in the city of Chicago. Founded in 1846 (during the Great Irish Famine), it was the first English-speaking parish in the city. The current church building was dedicated on Christmas Day, 1856. It is one of the few buildings to survive the Great Chicago Fire of 1871.

When the Irish came to America, they came seeking political and economic freedom. However, the American dream was unkind to many and many spirits were broken through deprivation and despair. In 1893 an exhibition of Irish artefacts known as the Columbian Exhibition went on display in Chicago. It brought with it such rare treasures as the Tara Brooch and the Ardagh Chalice among others. It helped to rekindle the Irish spirit. In the years that followed, 1912-22, the then pastor William McNamee commissioned artist Thomas O'Shaughnessy to redecorate the church interior in a Celtic Renaissance style, reflecting the rich heritage of those who worshipped there. The church building itself was designed in a Romanesque style with two steeples being added to the church towers in 1885. The taller Gothic tower represents the Church of the West. The Byzantine onion dome on the North tower represents the Church of the East. Together the steeples represent the universality of the Catholic faith.

Between the years 1912-22, O'Shaughnessy designed fifteen stained glass windows inspired by the Celtic designs of the book of Kells. The final windows which were done in an art nouveau style are installed in the eastern facade of the church and are a triptych entitled the 'Faith, Hope and Charity' windows.

In 1964, the church became the first Chicago building officially designated a landmark by the Chicago City Council. In 1977 Old St Patrick's was listed on the National Register of Historic Places.

In May 1996 the church was closed for an interior renovation recalling the Irish art renaissance of St Patrick's Church between 1912-22, characterised by O'Shaughnessy's design. The designs on the walls and ceilings are exact replications from the original designs. Inspired by the Book of Kells, an ancient illuminated manuscript, O'Shaughnessy's designs represent one of the only collections of Celtic artistry in the world.

When I first walked into this sacred space, I was speechless. I felt as if I was walking through the pages of an early Irish manuscript. I was in a 'Celtic Sistine Chapel'. Each panel was so delicately and beautifully presented. Though it was a newly renovated space, my thoughts were also of the early Irish emigrants who first came here almost two centuries ago. What were their thoughts as they knelt and prayed far from their townlands or parishes, searching the sea of faces that gathered to pray, hoping they might recognise a familiar face or a neighbour's smile. What was the life they left and what had the future in store for them?

To stand in such a place is indeed humbling, but to try and capture this moment in music is even more daunting. I felt *The Mass of the Celtic Saints* would find a proper home in this hallowed place. Set for Irish instruments, it would be sensitive to the moments of history that echoed and re-echoed in this church. I had to start composing...

The following year I travelled with a group of fellow musicians to perform the work, with my colleague and mentor Dermod McCarthy from RTÉ as narrator. On the night that we gathered for the first performance, I was acutely aware that 'Irishness' stretches far beyond the physical boundaries of the Atlantic coast or the Irish sea. Here were hundreds of people born in a distant land but as proud of their heritage as anyone born in Belfast or Bantry back in the 'old country'. Filled to capacity, the night was alive with the spirit of Ireland. It was a moving night. I am sure that the Chicago-born Irish corner of Heaven celebrated in style, and I have no doubt that in the midst of them was Jack Durkin, whose passing had prompted the ancient Celtic practice of hospitality to find life once again, and found a home for some new Irish music.

Allelu, alleluia
Allelu, alleluia
You will shine like bright stars for all the world to see
Offering to the world, the word of life
The gift of majesty
Allelu, alleluia
Allelu, alleluia

SACRED STORY
We tell the Sacred Story
We sing the glory of yesterday
We tell the Sacred Story
One who has shown us,
The Sacred Way

SACRED STORY

Sacred Story

*I*n 1996 I was commissioned by the Christian Brothers in Ireland to write a work for the forthcoming Beatification of their founder, Edmund Ignatius Rice. It was my biggest task to date and I greatly admired the trust placed in me by the Brothers. Since I had not been educated by the Christian Brothers, I knew very little about their founder, so I spent a considerable amount of time researching the life and times of Edmund Rice. What I uncovered was a remarkable story which I tried to weave in and through the music I was to write.

Edmund Rice was born in 1762 in Callan, County Kilkenny, into a land of great suffering. The Penal Laws being enforced, it was a time of great persecution, deprivation and religious oppression. Against this background the young Edmund Rice grew up, in a Gaelic heartland with all the traits of ancient Irish tradition.

In 1778 Edmund joined his uncle running the successful family shipping business which had developed trading links with England, the Continent and especially Newfoundland. Here in Waterford he met Mary Elliot, the daughter of a business man, and in 1785 they were married. At twenty-three years old Edmund had become a successful businessman with a loving wife and promising future. Four years later tragedy struck. While expecting her first child, his wife went into premature labour due to a fall from a horse. She died at child birth and the baby, christened Mary Rice, was handicapped. One can only imagine the intensity of grief that was carried in the heart of Edmund Rice. There is no doubt that the death of his beloved wife and the birth of his little daughter had a profound influence on Edmund and was to radically alter the course of his life.

His quotation, 'Cast all your cares into the arms of Divine Providence', found reality in the decisions that Edmund Rice was about to make. It could be said that the brokeness of his little daughter served as a prism through which he saw the wounded and broken society all around him – ignorance, wretchedness and illiteracy. Without dignity, most people lived in great destitution.

Edmund Rice became acutely aware of such pain. He sold his house along with his thriving business and established a school for Waterford's neglected in an old stable. What was his driving force? A desire to live the gospel of Jesus with the poorest of the poor. In embracing poverty he experienced the loneliness of misunderstanding, and yet with great zeal he worked to perfect his own form of education and care for those who were without, and there were many. Central to an education system that seemed far ahead of its time was the importance of the spiritual life which he sought to develop in all who came into his care. Realising this could not be done alone he invited others to join his way of life and to give their lives in the service of God's poor.

In 1809 he and his companies were invested with the habit of religion, but it was not until 1822 that his order was approved in Rome and Edmund Ignatius Rice became Superior General – from this congregation grew also the Presentation Brothers. He would guide his Brothers until six years before his death. In August 1844 Edmund Rice was called to his heavenly reward. On the 6th of October 1996 Edmund Rice was declared Blessed.

The *Sacred Story* collection was first performed at the Irish national celebrations in October 1996 at the National Basketball Arena in Tallaght, Dublin. A few weeks before I had been invited to Rome to attend the Beatification ceremony but also to perform at a special concert given the night before at the magnificent Paul IV indoor arena at the Vatican. The music presented at the concert was drawn from all over the world where Edmund Rice's communities were working. I was to perform a selection from *Sacred Story* with a group of my musicians and the Abbey Singers from Kilkenny. En route to the concert, the bus we were travelling on collided with another vehicle and I found myself thrown headlong into the dashboard of the bus. I feared I was seriously injured and that my composing days were drawing to a close. I was taken to the Santo Spirito Hospital in Rome where it was discovered that I had three broken ribs, a fracture and a number of lacerations. I was advised to quit singing for at least twenty days. In my dilemma, I decided that this was the 'other' miracle needed by Edmund Rice to help his cause for sainthood. I kindly dispensed myself out of the hospital and got a lift to the concert hall. Greeted like a long lost son, I performed, though sitting and in a lot of pain. As I was about to walk off stage, one of my satirical friends kindly whispered into my ear, 'Break a rib'. I am sure I heard Edmund Rice chuckle in the background!

And from the earth is fashioned
the hope of life renewed
In human heart embodied,
The God of love and truth.

SING A SONG

Sing a song to the Lord's holy name
May the wonders of God be proclaimed
Sing a song to the Lord now acclaim
Alleluia, alleluia.

THE CLOUDS' VEIL

Sing A Song

As I write this book, I am currently engaged on a concert tour at home in Ireland. The tour is taking us to all kinds of places throughout the country and thankfully has enabled many charities to benefit from hugely successful 'houses' – as they say in the business!

Working with professional musicians, singers, lighting and sound people has enabled me to present my music in a way that is both different and accessible. The marriage of the aural and the visual within a sacred space (as most of our concerts are in churches or cathedrals) works beautifully and allows people to experience sacred music in a new and captivating way.

It is important to meet with people afterwards, particularly those who have travelled long distances to be with us. I am always intrigued by the variety of people who attend – young, old, musician, non-musician, church-goers and non-practising alike. There is something about Irish music that appeals to the human soul – perhaps because of its pathos and heart-rending melodies. But I am also constantly amazed by the power of music to heal and to bond. I could fill an entire book on this subject, particularly about the power of music to touch the human spirit and to move us in our deepest areas of pain and loss.

Music builds bridges and makes conversations that need no words. It provides the space for people to stand open and vulnerable, knowing that it is possible to lift the soul to a better place. In music we often talk about the importance of melody but another important element that should not be forgotten is harmony. Harmony adds depth and richness and will colour a melody in many different ways. Meeting so many individuals after performances I too am made aware of the great richness and diversity among people. Music makes connections and is a vehicle by which conversations and even life-long friendships begin. Music creates bonds that exist far beyond the limits of time. It evokes memory and can stir up feelings we once thought lost and perhaps forgotten. It links us with the past, easing melody from memory.

When we come together in a liturgical setting to celebrate our faith, music can also build bridges and minister to people's needs. Sadly, if the liturgy is poor and the music is not complimentary, we do a great disservice to those who gather. Sometimes we need to move from complacency to change. I am often reminded of the story of St Teresa of Ávila who led her sisters in dance and song around the monastery chapel so that they might rediscover their desire to praise God. I often wonder if I suggested the same at a Sunday gathering would I be led away by men in white coats! However, I am rediscovering more and more as I perform that many people are like St Teresa at heart. They want to sing and dance within our sacred spaces but are often not empowered to do so.

Music is a gateway where strangers and friends alike can join in a common celebration of life and faith. I am trying to understand why a packed audience will sit for two hours on wooden seats and still want more, and yet our Sunday celebrations can seem so lacking.

A number of years ago I spent some time with the American contemporary composer, John Michael Talbot. I had gone to stay with his community as I was eager to discover the secret of his success in the music business, but I soon realised that he too wanted to learn from me – to explore the ancient Celtic church and its notion of community. In ways I couldn't imagine, he taught me in those early days about the wealth of the tradition that I come from but knew little about at that stage. I believe that music plays a central role in building the Christian community and this is what I experienced in the Little Portion Community of John Michael Talbot. Such music helps us to celebrate God's presence among us and thereby builds community.

There is a word in the Irish language known as _seisiún_ – meaning session. To an outsider it means an assembly or a coming together for an activity but in Ireland it embodies much more. It is a colloquialism for a 'celebration', a time for letting one's hair down to enjoy the blessings of life, and music is central to such a gathering. If you ever play at an Irish session with traditional musicians you will become aware quite easily that there is an underlying sense of belonging and support – 'if you play, you stay'. To harness such energy and soul music for the praise of God would transform our liturgies and heal and uplift our communities. Last night in concert, I stopped the singers and musicians in mid-song. The audience continued singing, completely oblivious to the halted voices and players. Why? Because caught up in their own desire to sing, they felt comfortable enough to continue. They were not inhibited and wanted to be there.

'Sing a Song to the Lord' was written for a community to celebrate – the community of Birr, County Offaly, in the midlands of Ireland, who celebrated the life and times of their local saint, St Adomnán. Born *c.* 628 he was a descendent of St Colmcille's grandfather. In 679 he became the ninth abbot of Iona but in Birr he is remembered for the enacting of Adomnán's Law, a law passed for the protection of women, children and clergy, especially during warfare. Up to this time, women and children were sent into the front lines of battle carrying munitions and were most susceptible to danger. Known as a peaceful character, he was a noted scholar and is the author of *The Life of Colmcille*. It was written in Iona where he died in 704. We may wonder at how such connections are made but I have no doubt that it is music that has offered a bridge over time and space, forging a link with past that may otherwise lie forgotten.

Day by day we count on God's blessings
Day by day we seek for God's strength
Day by day may love be our lesson
May our wonder of God have no end.

MO GHRÁ THÚ
Mo ghrá thú a Thiarna
Mo neart thú
Mo ghrá thú a Thiarna

MOLAISE

Mo Ghrá Thú

I was sixteen years old when I first heard the music of the great Irish composer Seán Ó Riada. As is the custom with many Irish young people, my brothers and sister and I spent our summers at what was known as the *Colaiste Gaeilge* – or Irish summer colleges – where one spent a month learning the Irish language, culture and music. I remember such days with sweet memories. The particular college that we went to was set in the east Cork village of Castlemartyr and was the Alma Mater of my father.

Each Sunday the group of students would gather to celebrate the Eucharist and central to this celebration was of course the music and songs of our tradition. For me the music of Ó Riada had a lyrical yet numinous quality that stirred my soul. These were the first days of my experiencing traditional instruments alongside the church organ. From that time on, I firmly believed that such instruments and such music had a rightful place in sacred surroundings.

This was the music that reached the soul and offered solace and comfort to many heart-rending or joyful situations. It was the music of the people, earthed in real life experience. It was during this period of my life that I was also introduced to the music of Donegal, and especially the music of the Irish speaking area in the north-west of the county. Through the music of Máire Brennan and her brothers, sisters and uncles, I entered the world of Clannad – an Irish traditional group whose name would be linked with platinum albums, film scores and superstars in later years.

What was it about their music that stirred something primal deep within me? The combination of voices, instruments and musical material seemed to touch a spiritual vein. It was mystical and majestic with haunting echoes of other days. It was 'the sound' that I yearned to offer in a spiritual setting, perhaps because I knew it was part of what we were and are.

I was to perform myself later in the *Amharclann* in Gweedore – the same theatre that had been a birthing ground in the early years of Clannad. Being in Donegal helped me to understand how landscape has a music all of its own. The song of the tide, the cry of the curlew, the call of the wind – all sounds that create a song of their own which inspires, haunts, heals and cries out. Such music is food for any composer's soul. It is such a place that inspired my writing of 'Mo Ghrá Thú'. In the translation of this Psalm 18 setting, God is likened to a rock, a fortress, a shield. It offers a sense of security and strength and is written as a devotional song.

Some years after I had recorded this piece, another beautiful voice of the Donegal Gaelthact – Aoife Ní Fhearraigh – recorded it on her debut album, simply titled *Aoife*, and the producer was none other than Máire Brennan of Clannad, who had now begun her own solo career. The track was sensitively recorded and went on to feature on an American collection called *Celtic Spirit*. In all, this piece of music has appeared on seven different albums, much to my joy and surprise.

After I have been away and I am returning home to Ireland, I always like to get a view of the landscape as we sail through the clouds. Green, rocky and dotted with lakelands, its features have been around for millions of years, long before we ever set foot on the sacred soil. It holds many secrets. It has known famine, war, the ravages of time and the progress of modern civilisation. Yet it remains silent, strong and steadfast, something akin to the continuing presence of God, its creator, the God of this song.

Mo Dhia thú mo charraig, is mo dhídean;
Mo sciath, adharc mo shlánaithe, mo dhún
Glaoim ar an Tiarna dar dleacht moladh
Agus déantar mo shaoradh ó mo naimhde.

SAIL THE SOUL
Sail the Soul
May God safely guide us
Through all days...

Sail The Soul

As I have become more established as a liturgical composer I have received many commissions. A number of compositions are based on the life and times of saints in Ireland, particularly those known at national level or even the less well known ones at local level. Researching the lives of the ancient past has afforded many opportunities for reading old texts and gaining an insight into the life and times of such people.

In 1997 the 1400th anniversary of the death of St Columcille was celebrated in the Diocese of Raphoe, or Donegal, and the Diocese of Derry, as both have associations with the saint. Who was this great man and what was the legacy he left behind?

Columcille, meaning the 'Dove of the Church', was born in Gartan, Donegal, around 520-22. He came from a race of kings who had reigned in Ireland for six centuries and he himself was not far from royal succession to the throne. As was the custom, he was placed under the fosterage of a holy man at a young age. He studied under two men named Finian, the latter at his monastery at Clonard, County Meath. From there he went to the monastery at Glasnevin, Dublin, where he was eventually ordained under the guidance of a holy man called Mobhi. He spent the next fifteen years preaching and teaching in Ireland.

By the time he was twenty-five he had founded no less than twenty-seven monasteries, including those at Derry, Durrow and Kells. Columcille was a poet who loved fine books and manuscripts. One of the most famous books associated with him is the 'Psaltair' which was traditionally the Battle Book of the O'Donnell clan, his kinsmen, who carried it into battle. This Psaltair is the basis for one of the most famous legends of Columcille. It is said that

Columcille was so anxious to have this book that he locked himself away and spent a whole night transcribing the book by hand. He was discovered by another monk who reported it to his superior. The scriptures were so scarce at that time that the abbot claimed the copy, but Columcille refused him until he was obliged to do so under protest on the abbot's appeal to the High King Diarmuid.

This was a turning point in Columcille's life. Legend has it that after the bitter feud which followed, in which many were slain, Columcille experienced a profound conversion, so filled with remorse was he when he realised how many were slain in the battle. Though he loved his homeland deeply, he vowed to become an exile and preach the Gospel elsewhere.

In 563, he and twelve companions crossed the Irish Sea in a coracle, a local boat made from animal hides and pitch. They landed eventually on a deserted island now known as Iona (Holy island). It was here on this tiny island off the Scottish coast that Columcille began his work. In time Iona was to become the heart of Celtic Christianity and led to the conversion of the Scots and Northern English.

It was from Iona that many other settlements were founded, while Columcille himself centred his ministry in the Scottish isles. It is believed that he anointed King Aidan of Argyll upon the famous stone of Scone which can be seen today at Westminster Abbey. He still maintained a deep interest and great influence in the church of his native island. His biographer, St Adamnán, wrote of him: 'He had the face of an angel: he was of an excellent nature, polished in speech, holy in deed, great in counsel... loving into all.'

Although his name means 'Dove', in his earlier years he was stern and quick-tempered, but over the years he softened and became gentler in character. His chief virtue lay in the conquest of his own passionate nature.

On the 8th of June, 597, Columcille was copying out Psalm 34 and when he had reached the lines, 'They that seek the Lord shall not want for anything that is good', he said let 'Báithene complete the psalm'. Columcille died the next day at the foot of the altar. He was buried at Iona, but two hundred years later the Danes destroyed the monastery and his relics were taken to Dunkild in Perthshire, Scotland, in 849. His feast day is the 9th of June, the day he died.

When I was asked to write this piece, I set out for Gartan, the birthplace of Columcille, in the north-west of Ireland in Donegal. It is located near the coast and offers the passerby a beautiful vista. I was struck by the image of water that would be so central to the life and mission of Columcille. The piece is based on the nature of the sea, and the rhythm of the music takes on its own life. This piece has been used by many sea-faring communities, both at home and abroad. My work and travelling has subsequently brought me into contact with the Iona community and the work of Scottish composer John Bell, whose efforts at building and healing communities continues today in the footsteps of Columcille, who has been attributed with these final words:

Alone with none but thee my God
I journey on my way
What need I fear when Thou art near
O King of night and day
More safe am I within Thy hand
Than if a host did round me stand.

So Longs My Soul

So longs my soul
It longs for thee
So longs my soul
So longs my soul, it longs for thee, O God
And thy refreshing grace.

In The Quiet

So Longs My Soul

Researching for my MA at the Irish World Music Centre in the University of Limerick has without doubt broadened my musical perspective. My study of 'Ritual and Chant' brought me face to face with expressions of culture that were previously unknown to me – from the sacred songs of Burma, the mbere music of Nigeria, the Gregorian tradition of Europe, or the music of the Russian Orthodox Church, comes a beautiful insight into the beliefs and spirituality of their people.

Having the opportunity to look deeper into such cultures allows one to appreciate more fully the great diversity and richness of our world. If we take the time to learn another person's song, we are allowing ourselves the possibility to change our own lives.

Common to most traditions, including our own Irish tradition, is the importance of 'oral culture' – the handing on of music and verse using the human voice rather than the written text, which in many instances followed later. Like the oral tradition, culture was kept alive as one generation after another retold the story of their people through song and verse. Often these songs belonged to those who were 'oppressed' people, suffering through lack of education, opportunity or finance. Very often songs were sung in local dialects, with local traditions colouring the texts. Even in some religious songs traces of pre-Christian belief are found.

In some of the more isolated, rural areas of countries, the 'old songs' remained unchanged and untouched for years. It is only within recent years, with the affects of globalisation, that such traditions are in danger of being lost forever. In many cultures the connection between traditional song and dance was very important, but sadly, too, this relationship has diminished. In Ireland many folk songs were based on particular areas and sung by particular communities. Sometimes they took the form of ballads or folk songs that told a particular story, with the stress on the crucial situation. The story was told by letting the action unfold in event and speech and was told objectively, with little comment or intrusion of personal bias.

When people emigrated from their native country, as with so many Irish people, they took with them their ballads and folk songs. Many of these songs survived in isolated settlements where there was little competition from other art forms. Usually such themes as politics, history, satire and religion were included in the folk song. In many instances such songs were commentaries on the harshness of life, as can be seen in the folk ballads of Ireland or the Negro-spirituals of America. On further inspection it may be said that such songs were in fact a commentary on life itself as it existed during these times.

While studying at the Irish World Music Centre we were graced many times with singers and performers from other lands and cultures, and I was to discover how similar and yet different such music is to the music of my own people. What is amazing is how such music has survived down through the centuries and how in each new generation there are people who are learning to appreciate and rediscover such ancient jewels.

The song 'So Longs My Soul' is based on Psalm 42. The text is based on a traditional folk setting from Cornwall which I heard sung by an English folk singer. Such songs were the songs of the community when they gathered for prayer. This particular song I heard was taught by a blacksmith who was the leader of a small group of singers in a small village. When they came to church on Sunday they had their own particular style of singing, common to that particular area. The original musical setting had a unique vitality and energy. Rhythmically the music was very different to the Irish style of singing and yet it had a rare quality of its own. I often wonder at how texts can be transformed in different settings. Though the psalm texts remain the same since they were first prayed, various musical settings have been composed throughout history. Such music offers a window into how people worshipped in times gone by. What is clear is that very often in worship people incorporated their folk songs into their prayer using sacred texts. A notable example of this in Ireland is the collection of songs known as 'The Wexford Carols'. These are some of the oldest carols in Ireland, sung with music from the popular music idiom of the people of the seventeenth century.

In composing this piece I used the archaic language style in which the text was sung in old England, and married it to a contemporary music setting, thus linking two worlds. It may be a far cry from the village blacksmith of Cornwall but surely the sentiments expressed are one and the same.

As pants the heart for running streams
When heated in the chase
So longs my soul for thee my God
And Thy refreshing grace.

THE CLOUDS' VEIL

Even though the rain hides the stars

Even though the mist swirls the hills

Even when the dark clouds' veil the sky

You are by my side...

THE CLOUDS' VEIL

The Clouds' Veil

I am often asked which of my compositions do I prefer the most or am happiest with. Most artists, I believe, are never entirely happy with their creations, but one piece that has meant much to people is 'The Clouds' Veil'. I have seen this piece of music used in all kinds of situations and somehow through the power of grace, touch people's lives.

Its text is very much influenced by the ancient Celtic sense of dignity for the earth and all creation. A sense of sacredness of the earth, of the presence of the Divine, illuminating all things from the ordinariness of every day life.

The ancient Celts were very conscious of the world of light and the world of dark. Their year was divided into halves – the summer from May to October called *Bealtaine* to *Samhain* and the other half from October to May – the dark winter. The division of this year was sometimes marked by an old custom which was known as *Buaile*. The cows were taken up for grazing into the mountains, where the herders lived throughout the summer season. As winter approached the herds were taken down into the foothills for shelter.

These people had a great awareness of the journey from darkness into light. Such journeys were often marked with festivals and celebrations. The end of the seasons marked a significant time in the lives of the people, as if time was suspended between the darkness and light. Known as the Third Dawn, it was the place of promise, the place of dreams and hopes – the time of boundless possibilities – to leave behind the darkness of winter days and walk towards the light of Spring, with new hope and resolution. With the coming of Christianity this period settled comfortably into the Christian calendar – the period between All Souls /All Saints in November through to the feast of St Brigid's Day and Candlemas Day in February, with the birth of the Light of God, Jesus, at the times of the winter solstice, now called Christmas.

The presence of the Divine in the world surrounding us is not always easy to see. At times the darkness of our own limitations overshadows the presence of light. Many live in the darkness of poverty, in the darkness of addiction, in the darkness of debt or even in the darkness of loneliness where hope is not easily found. Yet at times it is only when we sit in darkness that we can fully appreciate the light.

In Ireland, the light can play subtle games with the landscape, often providing a magnificent kaleidoscope of colour and shadows. Rainbows dance across the foothills while the dew rises from the bogs. Often the light is clouded by the swirling mists and we loose our panoramic view. Often the clouds of discontent hinder us from seeing the bigger picture.

In 1997 I was asked to compose a piece of music for the re-dedication of St Aidan's Cathedral in Enniscorthy, County Wexford. This beautiful Cathedral was built by the architect A.W.N. Pugin in 1846 and its steeple towers majestically over this beautiful town on the banks of river Slaney. It is an area steeped in history and was the centre of the historical insurrection of the group known as The United Irishmen in 1798.

As I was preparing this commission sadness struck. My uncle Patrick, who had been a musical mentor of mine over the years, was killed tragically in a motoring accident. It was a sad and difficult time and the muse of composition that so often compelled me to write was absent. I felt numb and unable to sing.

One evening, after a day's teaching, I picked up my post as usual and enclosed was a sympathy card from a choir colleague. I was struck by the simple beauty of an old Irish prayer on the card which included the line, 'Even when the sun is veiled, remember God is with you'. The image stayed with me, as it was so close to how I was feeling, and I am sure similar to how many others who experience the sadness of loss in their lives feel. That night I sat down and wrote 'The Clouds' Veil'. As I wrote the lyrics many beautiful images came to mind and I realised how God can be disguised in the simplicity of nature's guise, always there, in the natural rhythm, but so often I didn't take the time to look with what the Celts called 'the inner eye', i.e. to see the things that are so often taken for granted.

Writing this book, I received the word that my publishers in the United States, GIA Publications, chose this song as the most appropriate piece to remember all who had perished and suffered in the attacks of September 11th, 2001. It was humbling to think that my words might bring some small comfort to the many broken and shattered lives. Little did I think on an autumn evening as I sat down to write this piece that it would reach so many people.

As I reflect on all the happenings since, I realise that it can be so difficult to see the sun beyond the clouds, especially when all seems so dark. But somehow, as people of the Resurrection, we must keep hoping and believing that God is by our side.

Even when the sun shall fall in sleep
Even when at dawn the sky shall weep
Even in the night when storms shall rise
God is by my side, God is by my side.

THE WEAVER
So who will weave into the night
The hope of one, who comes with light
Who will weave into this life
Hope in journey's ending
Hear our prayers ascending

LIGHT THE FIRE

The Weaver

One of the most treasured possessions we hold in Ireland is the Book of
Kells – one of the world's greatest manuscripts which consists of the four
Gospels of the New Testament. Written in Latin, it tells the story of Christ's
life, but the book itself has a dark and engaging history. It is not certain where
or when the book was written but it is suggested that it was begun before AD
797 to celebrate the second centenary of the death of St Columcille.

This elaborate book was covered in a golden cover encrusted with gems and
precious stones and was displayed only on special occasions. Because of
constant invasion and danger, the book was relocated several times and
unfortunately never fully completed.

It had 740 pages, or 370 folios, but only 340 folios have survived. Written
on calfskin, the hide was stretched and flattened and smoothed over with a
pumice stone. It is estimated that the skin of approximately over one thousand
calves was needed. The skin pigments were bound by using the eggs of geese,
with their feathers making excellent quills. Various ingenious methods were
used to obtain the colours needed, for example, to obtain the colour black, soot
was used. However it wasn't always so easy and many colours proved difficult
to obtain. Some of the colours had to be found in distant lands, such as the red
hue, which was extracted from the pregnant body of a Mediterranean insect
known as 'kermes' which was believed to be a berry by the Romans. Another
colour – a beautiful blue – came from a precious stone known as lapis-lazuli –
and could only be found in the mountains of far off Afghanistan.

When one views the Book of Kells, one cannot but be astounded at the standard of craftsmanship: innumerable designs, interlacing knots and threads interwoven so perfectly without beginning or end. It was so perfect that it was considered to be the work of angels. It is thought that four master illuminators worked on the Book of Kells, painting and writing on single leafs that could be added later to the book. They taught their apprentices how to work on less complicated tasks. Viewing the book, one sees the perfect symmetry, the curving, the use of colour, the repetition of design, the whirls and swirls.

The calligraphy has been described as exquisite, with the use of countless symbols to enhance the artistry. The use of animal motifs occur throughout the book. The page that denotes the Incarnation of Christ is full of imagery from the animal kingdom. The beginning of each of the Gospels is highlighted by large and intricate designs showing depth of mind and a reflective intellect.

Often when working on manuscripts the monks would make some comment in the margins of the book which in later years became a great source of information in detailing life at that time. This was not so, however, with the Book of Kells.

But what of its fearful history? It is believed that the manuscript was written in Iona around AD 807, but the monks fled the monastery after a Viking invasion and arrived back in Ireland. The monks settled in Kells, County Meath, but in 1006 it was stolen from the this monastery.

> The Great Gospel of Colmcille, the chief relic of the Western world was wickedly stolen during the night from the western sacristy of the great stone church of Cennanus on account of its wrought shrine. That Gospel was found after twenty nights and two months with its gold stolen from it and buried in the ground. (The Annals of Ulster)

For centuries afterwards the Book of Kells was kept and revered at the monastery of Kells until the mid-seventeenth century. In 1653, during a difficult period in Irish history, the Governor of Kells sent the book to Trinity College in Dublin for safekeeping. It is there since.

To view such a priceless treasure is always a spiritual journey for me – not alone to view the beauty of the art work and calligraphy but to stop and reflect on the minds of those who created such beauty. If indeed, as it has been suggested, it was the 'work of angels', from where have they drawn their inspiration? Without all the modern conveniences of communication and artistic capabilities, what led these people to the resources they used? What kind of mind-set created the perfect and yet intricate patterns that wove themselves into and out of the pages of this rare and holy book?

The piece 'The Weaver' is inspired by such beauty. On inspection of the book one can see how it is designed with beautiful interlocking and interlacing weavings. In this era the crafts person, the goldsmith and the artist were seen as a blessing on the community and the monastic communities placed great emphasis on such gifts.

Many priceless pieces of art have been discovered and recovered all over the country dating back over the centuries from this golden era of Irish Christianity. When I wrote 'The Weaver' there were various strands of thought at work. It begins with three sung verses The first verse for a solo singer, the second verse for a duet and the third verse for a trio. This was to represent the Trinitarian concept (Father, Son and Spirit) that was so prevalent in the early Irish Christian prayers. This was followed by an instrumental section, also in three movements. Woven in as a dance piece it works wonderfully. One of my abiding memories of this piece was in the ancient setting of Ballintubber Abbey, a renovated early Irish monastery in County Mayo in the west of Ireland. The occasion was a television broadcast for transmission throughout Europe. Used as an Offertory piece – where the gifts of bread and wine are carried to the altar on behalf of the community – the dancers wove a majestic and beautiful Irish dance, preparing the way for bread of the earth and the fruit of the vine to be blessed, broken and shared by all.

So who will weave into this night
The hope of one who comes with light
Who will weave into this life
Faithful love descending, rest in journey's ending.

THE SHEPHERD BOY
I was once a Shepherd Boy
Climbing to the hills
To a place where no-one knew
Where my heart was stilled

THE SHEPHERD BOY

The Shepherd Boy

I have always been captivated by the story of Patrick. Though only seeing glimpses of his life on the yearly feast of 17th March, I often wondered about the human story behind the old man with the beard and crozier, with staff and shamrock.

When in 1999 I was commissioned to write a work for Siamsa na nGael at Chicago's Symphony Hall for St Patrick's Day 2000, I decided to explore the life and story of the boy Patrick. My research challenged me to present the human story of a young boy snatched from a secure, familiar environment and taken to a far off land to experience hostility and hardship. Who was this man and what impact had his life on our land?

Patrick was born probably around AD 400 in a town called Banaventa Berniae where his father, Calpornius, was a Roman official and a deacon who enjoyed noble status. In a violent raid, Patrick and many others were taken captive and he found himself in an undeveloped rural and hostile environment. He was probably around sixteen years old when this occurred. He became a shepherd in an area known as Foichoill near the western shores of Ireland. It is here that he learned to commune with nature, through isolation, hardship and loneliness, but also where the boy-Patrick discovered his God. Surrounded by a people who worshipped Pagan Gods, Patrick's faith grew as he learned to appreciate the virtues of his Christian belief.

It was this struggle with human misery and isolation that compelled me to read and research more about the life of this young man. In his writings, which are known as his 'confessions', Patrick tells us that he finds himself 'truly humiliated by hunger and nakedness' (C27:22-23). After six years he is then guided by the 'hand of God' to run and escape. Eventually after three days on the run he boarded a ship that eventually takes him back to his people.

During this period Patrick encounters the presence of God through dreams and visions and eventually after some years, he details a 'vision of the night' in which he saw a man called Victoricius coming as if from Ireland with countless letters, handing him one of the letters which contained the 'voice of the Irish' – saying 'we request you, holy boy, that you come and walk once more among us'.

Patrick befriends the native Irish, their clans and chieftains, and begins to spread the Christian message and Gospel to many areas. It was not an easy task but one which beheld great human struggle and suffering, including the slaughtering and capturing of many of his followers by slave traders who continued to wreak havoc throughout the land. Yet Patrick remains completely trusting of God – 'I pray God that he may give me perseverance and to grant that I may be a faithful witness to him' (C25:14-15). Patrick's active life was over by about 480.

The more I researched the life of this man, the more I desired his story to be known. I called the work 'The Shepherd Boy' and had a young boy soprano, Tim Coalter, playing the young Patrick while an elderly gentleman played the senior Patrick. In America we were wondering who could best play this role. I wanted someone who would narrate the story with pathos and conviction. I was introduced to Gregory Peck, the legendary screen actor whom I had seen many times over the years on stage and screen. For two days we worked on the script and with great empathy he made the text his own. I could see that he too was moved by the life of the one he was about to narrate. On stage the striking contrast between the young boy soprano and the eloquent gentleman was inspiring as it helped to underline the trial and triumphs of the life of Patrick. Gregory Peck's distinctive voice fell on a silent audience, recounting the confessions of one who knew both suffering and joy in this ancient land.

One of the most stirring pieces for me in the work is based on the betrayal of Patrick by those close to him who had become envious of his progress and achievement. Simply called 'Betrayal', I wrote the piece for the button accordion, which to me is one of the most heart-rending instruments, full of pathos. I was very fortunate to have the great Irish-American musician John Williams play, coupled with the sensitive whistle playing of Dominic Trumfio, one of the finest musicians that I know. At the rehearsal the night before, when the two musicians had played the piece, a silence descended as the members of the orchestra stopped and clapped, so moved were they by the playing. I stood at the back and wept.

On the night of the concert, my father and mother sat proudly in the Symphony Hall in Chicago. As a young boy my father had swam in the waters of Red Barn in Youghal Bay on the east coast of Ireland. It was into this bay that Gregory Peck had sailed many moons ago while filming *Moby Dick*. My father had heard of this great actor from the local people, but now here he was before him, recounting the life and times of a young shepherd boy. Life has mysterious turns and untold blessings. Later when I spoke to Mr Peck about the film, he remembered his days in Youghal vividly.

I cannot now think of Patrick without remembering the old man and the young boy. One life beginning and one life ending and the words that say:

Et hari est confessio mea

Antequam moriar...

(And this is my confession before I die...)

PILGRIM SONG
Alleluia Alleluia Alleluia Alleluia
Alleluia Alleluia Alleluia Alleluia

LIGHT THE FIRE

The Pilgrim Song

Pilgrimage is an important spiritual event in many of the great world religions. It has always been part of the search for the Divine. In Islam, the pilgrimage to Mecca, the hajj, is one of the five pillars of Islam. The Jewish seder meal finishes with the blessing, 'Next year in Jerusalem'. To celebrate the millennium many old pilgrim paths were re-established throughout the Christian world: the great pilgrim sites of Santiago de Compostela in Spain, Chartres in France, and Guadeloupe in Mexico, to name but a few. In Ireland nine ancient pilgrim paths were re-developed for the year 2000, many highlighting the ancient routes of the great Celtic saints in the search for solitude and sanctity. Pilgrimage refers to both an external journey, usually taken on foot, and an interior journey which the great spiritual writers see as the 'desire to seek intimacy with God through contemplation and mystical surrender'. St Theresa of Ávila speaks of the soul making a journey to different rooms in the castle of one's spiritual life.

Psalm 84 speaks especially to the pilgrim who 'have highways in their hearts... Happy the people whose strength you are; their hearts are set upon the pilgrimage'. Church documents at various times refer to the Church on her 'pilgrim way'. It continues to be a pilgrim people on the journey to our heavenly home.

In the early Celtic Church pilgrimage took various forms. Some made the decision to live a life of permanent or voluntary exile. Such Irish saints as Colmcille, Brendan and Patrick lived so. There were also temporary pilgrimages where pilgrims would take 'time out' to follow a pilgrim route. The climbing of Patrick's mountain, known as Croagh Patrick, in County Mayo, existed even in pre-Christian times and was a sacred site, a holy mountain. It continues to be a popular pilgrim route today.

Living in exile was not easy and these same accounts written by the early Irish monks testify to the hardship of such a life. A poem by an unknown Colmán written on the continent to another Colmán wishing him a safe journey home to Ireland reads:

> So, since your heart is set on those sweet fields
> And you must leave here
> Swift be your going — heed not any prayers
> Although the voice be dear.
>
> Vanquished are you by love of your own land
> And who shall hinder love
> Why should I blame you for your weariness
> And try your heart to move?
>
> God give you safe passage on the wrinkled sea
> Himself your pilot stand
> Bring you through mist and foam to your desire
> Again to Ireland...

Perhaps it is difficult for us to grasp the meaning of such sacrifice today where, with the global culture that exists, we can move quite easily from one place to another. In the past, such a decision to leave one's own home was a tremendous sacrifice. The historian Patrick Corish writes:

> In this society where a man's status as a citizen was quite normally accepted only within the boundaries of his 'tuath' (locality) the idea seems to have emerged quite early that self-exile from one's nature community was the greatest asceticism, short of physical martyrdom, which a Christian could undertake.

Leaving home in voluntary exile was a response to Christ's call to leave all and follow Him, where the words of Abraham in the Old Testament were taken to heart: 'Go forth from thy country and from thy people, and out of thy father's house and come into the land which I shall show them'.

In the Irish texts, the 'interior pilgrimage' was also of vital importance. The physical journey is the evidence and the catalyst for the inner journey. At the heart of the Celtic idea of pilgrimage is the inner journey of renewal, repentance, resurrection and rebirth. Pilgrimage was the outward expression of an inner change.

I wrote 'Pilgrim Song' while reflecting on the life of one Irish saint who exiled himself far from these shores. The story is told that in a little village in

Kerry, off the south-west coast of Ireland, a farmer was returning home one night when he saw a strange glow in the sky. That night, believe it or not, it was said that thirty of his cows gave birth to thirty calves. The farmer believed that such a bountiful gift was not meant for him but for someone special. That same night, a young boy was born in the village of Ardfert. His name was Brendan and he was placed under the care of a great holy woman called Idé or Ita. She was his *anam-chara* or soul friend, as was the tradition of the time, i.e. that such people would have a mentor to offer advice, guidance and sound spiritual leadership.

After years in her care, Brendan longed for days for contemplation with God in new surroundings. The sea beckoned him and he left his homeland and set sail to unknown destinations. In a voyage revisited by the navigator Tim Severin, it was thought that Brendan and his crew sailed the Atlantic and eventually reached Newfoundland, long before Christopher Columbus discovered America. His song on the sea was a song of joy and hope with the great ocean opening before him. I wrote this piece in traditional Gaelic style with an instrument called a bodhrán – one of the earliest percussion instruments found in Ireland. It has become a favourite among Irish congregations, but perhaps the greatest tribute to the piece occurred while I was celebrating a Mass for people with special needs in a community in the south of Ireland.

When the musicians and the choir began to sing the 'Pilgrim Song', a young man in the assembly stood up and began to dance and sing at the top of his voice. Soon he was joined by his colleagues and, with great freedom and without any inhibitions, danced with joy in the presence of God. It was a moving and most profound example of 'delight in the Lord'. As I sat and smiled to myself, I hoped and believed that in the 'Kerry' section of heaven, St Brendan and his sea-faring friends were doing the same.

Glory to God in the highest heaven
Peace to God's people, God's people on earth
Glory to God in the highest heaven
We sing in jubilation at the Saviour's birth

COME TO THE FEAST DIVINE
Will you come to the feast Divine
Bread from the earth and fruit of the vine
Come and taste this heavenly wine
Welcome the lost and the stranger,
Come to the feast of the Angels

IN THE QUIET

Come to the Feast Divine

I am often struck by the relevancy of early Celtic tales and stories for our world today. Though separated by centuries of development, technology and theology, there was much wisdom in ancient Celtic thinking which I believe grew out of a certain humility that acknowledged the presence of the sacred in all things. The sacredness of the earth as the home of the Divine commanded a respect and encouraged wonder and awe in the heavenly presence.

For such people the natural and supernatural were inseparable. They nourished themselves with food from the earth but sought the food of the 'other world' also to sustain them in times of trial and tribulation. I am always touched by the following story from our ancient collections.

One day, Connla, Son of Caomh Ceádchathach, the reigning High King, was standing on the great hill of Uisneach in County Westmeath in the very heart of Ireland. Suddenly, there appeared before him a beautiful women dressed in rich garments and fine jewellery. She recited a poem in which she explained that she came from Tír na nÓg – the Land of Eternal Youth – where there was no ageing or decay. She had fallen in love with the young Connla and she had come to invite him to return with her.

Connla fell completely in love with the girl as she recited the poem. The words fell like sweet honey from her lips. With all his heart he desired to return with her to Tír na nÓg, but he remembered that when his father died he would inherit his kingdom. He would be king. So, he told the beautiful young girl that sadly, he could not accompany her back to her land.

With heartfelt sadness she turned to leave, but before going she handed Connla a beautiful red apple, the sacred food of Tír na nÓg.

Connla was very downhearted when she departed and for a whole month he pined for her. Every time he thought of her he would take a bite out of the apple, but though he continued to eat it, it never diminished. He realised he was changing, his attachment to this world, its riches and promises, was decreasing. Matters of immense importance became less so – such a world receded in his mind.

Another month passed and once again Connla stood on the Hill of Uisneach. Suddenly the beautiful young girl appeared and invited him to go with her. This time there was no hesitation as she took him by the hand and led him to the seashore. There before the eyes of all they boarded a crystal boat and set sail for Tír na nÓg, the Land of Eternal Summer.

In the Western world we so often nourish the body and the intellect but so often neglect to nourish the soul. Many search but are not sustained by what they find. At the heart of the Christian tradition is the Eucharist through which the kingdom of heaven is extended to earth. Each week Eucharist is celebrated as communities gather in rural parishes, cities, hospitals, prisons and such places. It is an acknowledgment of the life and presence of God in the local community.

In distant times such celebrations were outlawed in Ireland so the people took to the hills and mountains to celebrate in secret. They gathered at 'mass rocks' amid the woodlands, rocks and hillsides. These became their cathedrals of trees. In the changing of the seasons the mystery of God was manifest. Such surroundings, though dangerous and in secret, were natural to a people who knew God to be present in the ordinary, familiar surroundings of every day life. Many beautiful hymns and prayers have been written about the Eucharist in Irish spirituality – the food for the soul. One such prayer is captured in the story of the old man who has to go in search of a priest in the middle of the night for his wife who was fatally ill. The priest returns with him bringing Holy Communion. As they ride on horseback through the night the old man begins to pray that his house will be a worthy dwelling place for the Lord who is about to enter his home.

I wrote 'Will you come to the Feast Divine' after reading a text from an early Christian writer from the second century, who urged the faithful to 'make of their hands a humble manger to welcome the Eucharistic Christ'. There is something sacred about open hands awaiting the Bread of Heaven; hands of hard labour, hands that hold children, hands that join in prayer now opened in welcome and hospitality. This piece was written for the community of St Mary's Cathedral, Winnipeg, in Canada, whose open arms of hospitality and friendship have blessed my life. In such a multi-cultural setting, which includes many Irish emigrants, the Christian notion of service is lived each week by those who gather to celebrate the Lord's day. In the midst of snow and ice, with temperatures of minus seven degrees, the welcome I received would melt any frozen wasteland. This song was first sung in Winnipeg on Christmas Day 2001, a suitable day to re-echo the sentiments written therein.

Make of your hands a humble manger
As once I came
Make of your heart a lowly stable
Love be born again.

Goltraí

Songs of Tears

THE DARKEST HOUR
The darkest hour
When land no more would flower
The darkest hour
When life's sweet taste was sour
Who knows the hour,
The darkest hour.

LIGHT THE FIRE

The Darkest Hour

In 1997 we celebrated the 150th anniversary of the Great Irish Famine. The last of the great famines of Europe, it left an indelible mark on the landscape of Ireland. In the late summer of 1845 a fungus, *phytopthora infestans*, struck Ireland for the first time, causing a potato blight. Since the potato was the main staple diet of the majority of the people who worked the land, its consequences were devastating. The blight persisted over a number of years. After the first year many who depended totally on the potato died, but in the following years many who were already living at a subsistent level were struck or else forced to emigrate. The landlords, whose workforce consisted mainly of poor labourers, cottiers and small landholders, had no one to maintain their holdings. After the famine almost four million of this group were either dead or gone.

There were many viewpoints as to why the famine occurred. But for those who were affected by it, it brought untold suffering that struck at the very heart of Irish life. Hunger, disease, eviction, death and emigration stalked the land. Places like Skibereen in Cork or Dingle in Kerry lost thousands in the harsh winters. Communities, once thriving, became places of blight and disease – areas to be avoided at all costs. In biblical terms, there were many who were too weak to bury their own dead.

In 1997 I was asked by the Irish Third World agency, Trócaire (meaning 'mercy'), to compose a piece of music to commemorate this sad event; the proceeds would go to their projects in the developing world. One project in particular involved the Ogoni people of the river states of Nigeria, who had suffered much displacement over the years because of the discovery of oil on their homelands. One voice stood out against a corrupt regime – poet Ken Sara Wiwa. He spoke out against the corrupt powers that sought to displace his people, but after a protest rally that went terribly wrong, and ended in the death of a protester, Sara Wiwa was convicted of murder and sentenced to death. His conviction led to many international protests, but despite the many international representations made on his behalf, his execution went ahead.

Where does one start in trying to compose a piece of music that is sensitive to the pain of such people? So often today we become desensitised to famine and war because it is, sadly, an everyday occurrence on our screens.

For my research into the famine I read the diary of an old parish priest in Galway who died in his 96th year. He told the story of how one Sunday morning he walked to the chapel to celebrate Mass and on his way he encountered the bodies of nineteen men, women and children in the ditches and strewing the roadside. Just inside the chapel gates lay a poor man clutching a small morsel of bread and making attempts to raise it to his mouth. He would bend his head, holding the bread between his knees to try and take a bite. He was simply too weak, however, and on his third attempt he toppled over. The old priest anointed the poor soul and he died tearing the dough with his nails.

This story haunted me for some time as I tried to write. How could the priest continue to celebrate with such pain and desperation around? Placing myself in his painful place I believe it would have been *my* darkest hour as people and community disintegrated around me. I am not certain that I would not have given in to despair. The pitiful sight of dying children is all too common in such circumstances. I titled the piece 'The Darkest Hour'.

In 1998 I was invited by the Ancient Order of Hibernians, an American based Irish group, to direct the music for their annual conference held at the Cathedral of St Paul's in Minneapolis. During the conference an exhibition of the Irish Famine was launched by the then Irish Ambassador and I was invited to perform 'The Darkest Hour'. In the exhibition I came across a painting which highlighted the plight of those who boarded the now infamous 'coffin ships' and tried to flee from the horror of death. One such group were those who landed at a small settlement known as Grosse Isle, off the coast of Quebec in Canada. The painting recounts the story of a group of Irish Sisters working at Grosse Isle. One day the Sister in charge called the Sisters together and informed them that word had come through that a ship was arriving from Ireland where a famine was raging, carrying many who were dying and diseased. The ship lay docked some miles from the shore and the Sister in charge asked for volunteers to journey out to the ship with her. She warned that the consequences may be serious as cholera was rampant. All the Sisters volunteered to go out to their fellow Irish brothers and sisters. All of the them, with the exception of one, contracted cholera and died later. There were approximately fifteen thousand people buried in Grosse Isle.

As I stood reflecting on paintings before me, I couldn't but think of the many, many stories that could be told by so many souls who boarded such ships to take them away from bitter agony to a supposed better life. For so many the story began and ended in places like Grosse Isle.

Singing 'The Darkest Hour' in the shadow of this painting, there are a series of echoes at the end of the composition. I wrote these lines into the piece deliberately, hoping that such echoes might traverse the boundaries of time and space to remind a people who died in silent, unknown corners of the world, that in their darkest hour, they were not forgotten.

Shall we sleep remembering the night that knew no end
When life's sweet hope was vanishing because we knew no friend
'Twas death we did befriend.

PIETA — THE SILENCE & THE SORROW
Who will come and share my sorrow
Hold my heart 'till wake tomorrow
Is there time that I could borrow?
Oh, oh, the silence and the sorrow.

ANCIENT WAYS

Pieta – The Silence & The Sorrow

For the past number of years I have been involved with religious broadcasting in Ireland, in the live broadcasts themselves and also as an adviser. Such work has taken me all over the country to many different locations, but my story about this particular piece of music takes me back to the Cathedral of the Assumption, Carlow, where I have worked for a number of years.

On the completion of the restoration of the Cathedral in 1997, the Holy Week services were broadcast on national television each day. On Good Friday night a special programme of reflection, song and interview titled *The Women Who Stayed* was presented. Based on the women of Jerusalem who stayed with Jesus until his death, the programme looked at the lives of five Irish women who have stayed in difficult situations offering love and support to those around them, despite loss, tragedy and suffering.

In writing music for such a programme, given that the particular day was Good Friday, I looked to the 'Pieta' of Michelangelo for inspiration. This piece of sculpture, which is found on St Peter's Basilica in Rome, is generally considered to be the masterpiece of Michelangelo's career. Mary, the mother of Jesus, holds the broken body of her son after he has been taken down from the Cross. Deeply poignant, exquisitely beautiful, it is more highly finished than his later works.

Looking at the Pieta, what really inspired my writing was two questions that I believed any mother in such a situation might ask – 'Is it possible we might borrow some more time together?' and, 'Is there anyone that knows the terrible pain in losing one's own flesh and blood?' The more I gazed on the image of the Pieta, the more these questions haunted me.

I wrote the refrain of the composition using these two questions but also in the style of the ancient keening songs of Ireland. Known in Gaelic as the _caoineadh_, such songs were sung as laments at the death of a loved one and had a particular musical style. More often than not the phrase 'O' or _Ochón_ was used to denote the pathos and sadness of the moment.

Having successfully performed this piece for the television broadcast, the song was consigned to my filing cabinet. On the 15th of August 1998, a little over a year after I last sang the song, a huge bomb exploded in the town of Omagh in the North of Ireland killing twenty-nine people and injuring and maiming hundreds. The loss of life and carnage has destroyed so many lives. It seemed that the words of this song were being relived all over again. Time stood still.

Some time later I was giving a recital one evening in Donegal with Aoife Ní Fhearraigh, a friend and fellow performer. I decided to sing 'Pieta – The Silence and The Sorrow'. When the concert was over I was approached by an elderly gentleman, a gentle soul who was upset and graciously asked me for the text of the song. This kindly man then told me that his brother had lost his wife, his daughter – who was carrying twins of seven months – and his granddaughter. They had died in the bombing of Omagh.

The shocking revelation of such loss was frightening. How could the hearts of those left behind bear so much suffering? Why should anyone have to bear such pain?

My only response to this man was to promise him that every time this song would be sung, I would remember the people of Omagh and their loved ones. As a tourist, it is easy to walk by the Pieta, to see it merely as a piece of sculpture without allowing its story to touch our lives. It is as easy as switching off when we become used to seeing violence on our screens. I was amazed at a recent statistic that said on average most young people have witnessed at least 13,000 deaths on television by the time they reach 20.

Since I wrote this song our world has become an even sadder place, due to the tragedies that stole so many lives in the United States of America and other fatalities around the world. For me one of the most poignant features of the Pieta is the contrast between the broken body of Jesus, bruised by hatred, and the compassion and gentleness of Mary who saw the dignity of the human body and embraced it with love. Perhaps a time will come when the Pieta will truly be appreciated for what it is – a symbol of loving compassion in the face of hatred and evil.

CRY TO THE DAWN
Cry to the dark to lift her mourning veil
Cry to the heart to break the binding chains
And from her tears will the waters wash the sands
To rid all fears for the dawn is now at hand
Oh who will seek to heal our land

SACRED STORY

Cry To The Dawn

In Ireland and especially in Carlow where I now live, it is possible to look out of your window and see the marks and remnants of history etched on the landscape. Carlow has a long and ancient history and boasts one of the largest Dolmens (an early Celtic burial site) in Western Europe, almost five thousand years old.

Another important historical feature of this town is Carlow College, which I have been associated with for a number of years. It is one of Ireland's oldest educational institutions, dating back to 1793, five years before Ireland's famous rebellion of 1798. Originally founded as a lay college, Carlow functioned as a college of the humanities and a seminary from 1793 until 1892. From 1892 until 1989 it was a seminary for the education of Catholic priests, but today it is a thriving third-level college studying Social Studies, Humanities and Applied Theology, with students from all over Ireland and beyond. The influence of Carlow College has spanned over 200 years of history. It educated such people as John England, whose writings remain a storehouse for the development of American Catholic theology, or the pioneering priests of Australia who ministered to and served some of the earliest settlers in this new land. Others included the poet Richard Dalton Williams and the impressionist artist, Frank O'Meara.

History was forged within the walls of this establishment with such speakers as the leading Irish politician Daniel O'Connell, or people like our own

James Doyle, the Bishop of Kildare and Leighlin, who worked tirelessly in defending the rights of Irish Catholics in the early years of the nineteenth century. Many others, too numerous to mention, followed in their footsteps, leaving their legacy in many corners of the world.

It was in the setting of Carlow College that I decided to record the collection *Sacred Story*, the college chapel offering such a beautiful natural acoustic for the style of music I had written. It seemed fitting in such an ambience since *Sacred Story* was based on the life of Edmund Rice, founder of the Christian Brothers in the eighteenth century.

'Cry To The Dawn' deals with the Ireland that was emerging after the Penal Days, the Ireland in which Carlow College and Edmund Rice lay their foundations. It was a land of shadows and pain, with much deprivation and degradation. Since the final collapse of the old Gaelic Order, the history of Ireland had been one of untold sorrow and political instability, where oppression became the norm.

The government of 1641 had decreed the absolute suppression of the Catholic religion in Ireland. Oliver Cromwell, an English general, engaged in a crusade of unrelenting tyranny for what he believed was the 'greater glory of God'. The land was taken from the native people and divided between settlers from overseas who were granted land in Ireland as reward for fighting for the Crown in various conquests. Cromwell's aim was the total suppression of the Catholic religion in Ireland. It was a system of apartheid which lasted for centuries.

Catholics were excluded from all public life and from education. It was forbidden to buy land, to obtain a mortgage, to rent or inherit land. When a Catholic landowner died, his estate could not pass to his eldest son but had to be divided equally among all sons, but if any son became a Protestant he automatically inherited all the land. No Catholics could join the army or vote, or be elected to Parliament. They could not keep a house worth more than £5. Priests were banished from the country and if they returned were liable to be hanged, drawn and quartered. Bounties were offered for the capture of the clergy and priest-hunting was actively encouraged. Mass was celebrated in isolated boglands, in the mountains, and most children were educated by wandering teachers in hedge schools.

Not long before I wrote this work I had travelled with a journalist friend, Heather Parson, to war-torn Bosnia. Heather was researching for a book she was writing and because of a connection we were able to travel to some of the devastated areas. Margaret Heckler, the then American Ambassador to Ireland was also in the group. What I saw and encountered I was not at all ready for. Writing the above passage about the Penal Days brought me face to face with some of the scenes that we witnessed in Bosnia. In ways it was apocalyptical, as we drove silently and without any lights through deserted villages through the night. Many nights I lay awake listening to towns and villages being shelled. In one refugee camp, where many women had been brutally raped, young children became the responsible adults caring for shell-shocked and traumatised mothers. Old people slept in the open fields and ditches. Children as young as fourteen had to join the army and experience the horrors of the front line. In one hospital we visited, seven stories were shelled, so on the ground floor open operations were taking place on the corridors. I remember the innocent faces of little children with limbs torn by bullets. I am forever haunted by such images.

Yet, as in the days of Edmund Rice there were those who sought reconciliation not revenge, those who sought peace not war. I encountered much goodness and unselfishness as volunteers worked every possible hour to bring some consolation and comfort in this living hell. I remember celebrating Mass in the basement of a hospital, surrounded by the wounded and dying. It was a humbling experience that puts the full meaning of the passion, death and resurrection of Jesus into perspective.

In the midst of great suffering God has always raised up those among us who are a countersign to the world of hate and revenge, people whose names are known to all. But there are also those whose names will never be written in the history books of the world – the little people who give their lives quietly and unassumingly to show a different face of humanity, they who, like Edmund Rice, have learned to 'cast all their cares into Divine Providence'.

Sometimes on a summers evening I like to walk around the grounds of Carlow College. Nestling in the grounds is the old graveyard where past pupils and staff members lie. Some of their stories will never be known . The sacrifices and service, the silent witness that many gave, at home and in far distant lands because they yearned to offer a better way to the world they knew.

Recently when I was approached to have *Sacred Story* performed in Australia, I thought of all those who once walked the halls of this college, and left our shores to sail down to the New Land, that in singing these songs, they too, might be remembered for writing and living their own sacred story.

Cry to the dawn, will it ever meet the day
Cry to the lost, their forgiveness now we pray
And through her time, the moon her watch she keeps
And all who lie in the fields of death, they sleep
Who will heal the soul who weeps?

PITY THEN THE CHILD
Pity then the child whose heart is ever wild
Who wonders at the earth, the sky, the sea
Tender is the child whose heart it knows no guile
Who'll gaze the face of God eternally.

SACRED STORY

Pity Then The Child

While I was writing the music for *Sacred Story* I was determined to include the story of Mary Rice, the daughter of Edmund Rice. As I have mentioned previously, Mary was born prematurely due to the fall of her expectant mother from a horse. For Edmund Rice, the tragedy of losing a young wife was made even more heartbreaking on the realisation that the little child was born disabled with special needs. In the Irish tradition such children were called *daoine le Dia* (God's people) and great reverence and respect was shown them.

Edmund Rice showed great love and care for his fragile daughter. The precise nature of her handicap is not known, but it is generally believed that it was a mental handicap. It is interesting to note that Edmund Rice remains silent about this chapter of his life. His thoughts and reactions he kept to himself, but there is no doubt that he took solace and comfort in his spirituality and faith. Perhaps it could be said that the brokenness of his young daughter served as a prism through which he saw the wounded and vulnerable children around him. For me, writing 'Pity then the Child' was a composition that was more than 'Mary Rice'. It was a song for all children, from all ages, especially those who continue to have no voice, no rights, no home, no parents, no love, no food, no hope, no tomorrow.

Even as I write this I am aware that many children suffer though the evil of slavery. There are millions of people in bonded slavery today – more than were taken out of Africa during the slave trade. Known as 'debt bondage', it exists where a person's labour is used as repayment for a loan and affects an estimated ten million people without impunity.

Children as young as five years old work long hours to provide some money for a meagre existence for their families. We are all only too aware of the horrific scenes from forgotten orphanages in Romania and Siberia where even the most fundamental of needs – human touch – is deprived.

Writing this song came at a particularly difficult period in the history of the Catholic Church in Ireland. A number of allegations had been made about the physical and sexual abuse of children and sadly such allegations were true. They were dark and difficult days for the Church, but particularly for the victims and their families.

The initial steps of healing for any victim occurs in the acknowledgment of guilt, by the perpetrators of a crime, thus allowing the victim to move on. Many lessons have been learned from these sad situations and there is profound hope that innocent lives will rise to live, hope and dream again.

The first time this song was performed was at the Irish Celebration for the Beatification of Edmund Rice held in Dublin for an invited audience. I had decided that it would be appropriate to use sign language to fully express the sentiments of the composition and I began to work with a wonderful group of boys and girls from the Deaf and Dumb School run by the Christian Brothers in Dublin. I learned so much from these young people whose sensitivity to the text was inspiring. I deliberately wrote an instrumental section into the composition as at such a point the signing would stop as there were no words. It was as if the group had been 'excluded', for without words they could not sign as they were unable to 'hear' the music. Why was this done? To highlight the fact that there are many people, especially children, excluded in our world because of disability, colour, race or creed. Such an action was a statement in itself to highlight such injustices in the so-called 'developed world' today.

I can still see the eyes of politicians, clergy and other guests being visibly touched by these young people and children who stood in the place of Mary Rice. I believe there is something of this little girl in all our lives – a part that is vulnerable and broken which can only be healed by genuine love and compassion and a proper understanding of the Sacred Scripture, that unless we become like little children we shall not enter the kingdom of Heaven.

When trust lies not within
Who knows of your hurting
Who quenches your thirsting
He will hear your voice , will hear your voice
And answer deep within.

THE LORD IS MY SHEPHERD

The Lord is my shepherd , there is nothing I'll want

Nothing I'll want,

Fresh and green are God's rich pastures.

The Lord is my shepherd, there is nothing I'll want

Nothing I'll want

For God guides to restful waters .

IN THE QUIET

The Lord is my Shepherd

One of my favourite songs from the Bible is Psalm 23, commonly known as 'The Lord Is My Shepherd'. The image of the shepherd sheltering and taking care of their flock is one that offers comfort and consolation. I used this musical setting in my work about the life of Patrick in 'The Shepherd Boy' but throughout my life there have been many situations in which this Psalm has become even more real, through the people I have known as true shepherds.

In 1995 I was contacted by the Missionaries of Charity, the congregation founded by Mother Teresa. I had already come in contact with the Order in the United States, but now I was asked to give a four day retreat to a group of girls who had just joined the Order in their formation house in Birmingham.

To say that I was apprehensive to take on the role of retreat director is an understatement and this was further compelled when the Sister in Charge asked me to speak on the topic of 'humility'. However, I soon realised that ways of God are both wise and very different than we can sometimes imagine, as in saying 'yes' to the Sisters' request I was in fact allowing myself to attend a 'school of spirituality' that had much to teach me.

There were about twelve girls in the group and all from extremely varied and interesting backgrounds, but the compelling common denominator was a deep desire to serve God in the 'poorest of the poor'. Some of these women were very well educated and had privileged lives, but now they were preparing to begin a life of complete selflessness, poverty and prayer.

I tried to understand the courage of such a vocation where girls from a modern image-conscious world would leave all and don a simple sari, one of the very few possessions that they would call their own.

My lesson in humility was about to begin as I spent more and more time in the company of these girls. Some of them had come straight from Albania and their story made for compelling listening. Their country, the poorest in Eastern Europe, was in a state of chaos and the practice of the Catholic faith was forbidden. One of the girls told me that it had been 22 years since a priest had served in their village. The last one had died, taken into the mountains, his executors allowing him to read a page of his Bible before they stoned him to death.

I asked her where and how she had learned her faith and she told me that as they worked in the fields her father and mother taught the family their prayers in the form of songs. At night they would gather to pray but always with someone on the look- out. This particular girl had walked for two days to hear Mother Theresa speak in a nearby city. She told me her father had walked with her and cried the whole way home because he sensed his daughter had heard a 'different call' and would soon leave their mountain village. He was correct. Within a year she had left and joined the Missionaries of Charity.

I marvelled at the courage of this young woman from the hill country of Albania, now in the middle of the bustling city of Birmingham trying to cope with new surroundings, a new language and new people. As she spoke with love of her family and home, her tears flowed freely. She would return home for two weeks at the end of the year and then return to the Order. After joining it may be a long time before she may see her family again, depending on what part of the world she would be needed.

Her story was reiterated by the stories of the others and I began to realise the very small sacrifice I had incurred by taking up the Gospel call of leaving all to follow the Lord – so small in comparison to these girls. They showed a great sensitivity to the broken people they served – and from my experiences of their Houses in different parts of the world, the Gospel virtues of care and compassion are a vital part of their charism as a religious Order.

I had the privilege later of meeting Mother Teresa on a few occasions, but there was one particular time that has left an indelible mark on my memory.

On this particular occasion, among the small group that was meeting Mother Teresa, there was a young girl who had just lost her brother in a tragic accident. It was an emotional meeting, but I was deeply moved as this small frail little woman, who had just fallen and broken her ribs, knelt down and embraced the young girl to comfort her. Constantly using words of comfort and hope, she reassured this young girl that there was no need to worry, her brother was now 'at home' and was with God.

What touched me deeply was that I saw the humility of a frail little woman – a Nobel Prize winner, a friend of kings and queens, presidents and princesses – who was not afraid to show tears of compassion as she held a complete stranger in her arms and tried to comfort and console her, the same arms that have held the dying in the streets of Calcutta, and with the same reverence and dignity.

In the chapel of every house of the Missionaries of Charity throughout the world is a simple crucifix on the wall with the words 'I Thirst' written beneath. The words are taken from the last words of Jesus as he lay dying on the cross.

This has become the way of life of these women, to quench the thirst of a hurting world and to bring some dignity into the final moments of those who have lived without love. Like the true shepherd, they go in search of the lost sheep, and bring them home to restful waters.

Near restful waters God guides my soul
Revives my spirit, God makes me whole
Guides me on the right path, guides me on the right path
God is true to his name.

AVE MARIA AVE

Guide us on the journey

Show to us the way be our home of resting

Our comfort when we stray

Guide us in your wisdom and your blessings share

As we come rejoicing

Ave Maria, Ave.

IN THE QUIET

Ave Maria Ave

*I*n Irish spirituality, Mary the Mother of God has always occupied a very special place. The Gaelic name for Mary is Máire, but Mary had her special own title – 'Muire'. Down through the centuries Mary was revered with intimacy and closeness, her human rather than her heavenly qualities revered. As one of the bardic poets wrote, 'She is the woman of the house for all'. From about the fourteenth century the Rosary became an important prayer in the Irish tradition and sustained the Catholic faith when there was little else to do so during the times of terrible persecution and the Penal Laws.

Why was Mary so revered in Irish life? Possibly because of her understanding of the human condition. She too had suffered much, and her final humiliation was to see her own son die a criminal's death.

Ireland was a country that knew much pain and poverty, thus it was natural to turn to Mary. 'I have the good Mother of God for a sister,' wrote a thirteenth-century poet. But there was also the belief that it was possible that we ourselves might offer comfort to Mary herself. In some of the early Irish writings this theme was found. Blathman, an eight-century poet speaks 'to gentle Mary and calls on her, his beautiful Queen, that they might converse together to comfort her heart'.

Early Irish spiritual writings were full of images of Mary expressed in poetry and song. She was described as *'Tonn Clíona na Trócaire'*, a 'mighty wave of mercy' that would protect Ireland and her people in times of danger and strife. One poet wrote that to help him in his fight against sin, 'I must keep in my heart, the thought of the great injury and insult it was to Mary', such was the closeness to her .

It is interesting to note that suffering for its own sake or even as an act of self-redemption was not part of Celtic spirituality. It was only when it was associated with the sufferings of Jesus through Mary that it became fruitful. St Columcille wrote, 'If we are companions with Mary in her co-passion in the time of the passion, we will be her companions in co-rejoicing in the glory of God's Kingdom'.

It is probably in her 'mothering' role that many identified with Mary in the Irish tradition. Since the family unit was the centre of Irish life, so too was the Holy Family an inspiration and an aspiration for all families. Many traditions grew out of the belief that the Heavenly guests might make the journey to our earthly homes and may arrive unannounced. Even on Christmas eve it was possible that the Holy Family might pass on their journey to Bethlehem, and to show that they would be most welcome in Irish homes a candle would be lit in the windows to offer hospitality. Many folk songs refer to this belief – that Jesus, Mary and Joseph, the unseen guests, might call in the guise of a stranger. The door between the 'two worlds' was never closed.

Speaking of the 'other world' also showed the importance of Mary as an Intercessor, especially with her son, who would be appeased by her prayers. Many believed that Mary would have great power to influence her son at the day of judgement – the mother would always listen to the Son. 'He is to be pitied who praises not Mary,' wrote the poet Aonghus Ó Dálaigh in the sixteenth century, and as a ploy to enter into the Heavenly court, they remind Christ that they were related to Him, 'On the Mother's side', since claiming family ties was part of a great tradition in Ireland. Mary was 'the door of Heaven, the exaltation of the Apostles, the Praise of the Martyrs'.

I have written a number of pieces of music with Mary as the focus. In my own life, I grew up in a home where the family rosary was a part of everyday life and once a year we made our pilgrimage together to the National Shrine of Our Lady in Knock in County Mayo. As a student I spent a number of years working at the Shrine of Our Lady in Lourdes and I have visited other Marian shrines in my capacity as a priest. Such places of Marian devotion may be regarded with cynicism by some, but one cannot deny the great search for healing of heart and soul that so many yearn.

I remember one day hearing the confession of a man who wanted to return to his faith. It had been forty-four years since he had last received the sacrament. I was deeply moved by his honesty. It has been my experience that devotion to Mary serves as a signpost to finding Christ. I am struck by the words of the author, Anne Carr:

> To think of Mary today as a model of faith in the pilgrim church is to think of her as a
> model for all Christians, women and men, in the journey of faith. This understanding of
> Mary as a model of the Christian on the path from unbelief to belief, a model of the slow
> and often painful growth of faith as it discerns responsible action in the tangled web of
> human life in time, can truly represent the pilgrim church today. A new, fully human under-
> standing of Mary as the one who receives and communicates the grace of Christ in the Spirit
> corresponds with the description of the church as pilgrim and all of us persons in the com-
> munity that is on the way (Anne Carr, Mary Model Faith, p. 20)

'Ave Maria Ave' was written for the Marist Sisters in the North of Ireland. My
brief was that the piece should be accessible to all, especially to their co-
workers and those who work in the community with them. Perhaps in such a
request lies a lesson for all engaged in ministry – that our work and service
should allow the Gospel to be accessible to all.

Mary is a woman of few words in the scriptures, but I have no doubt that
her human compassion and supporting presence were the backdrop which gave
courage to her Son as he set on the road of life. Perhaps the final words are best
left to those early Irish writers who very clear whom Mary was for them:

Is tú mo réalt eolais,
Ag dul romhan ann 's gach bealach
A's ar sliabh na ndeor
Go mbudh tu mo charaid.

(You are my star of knowledge,
when troubles rend me,
On the mountain of tears,
O defend me.)

THERE IS A PLACE
There is treasure in our fields
There is treasure in our skies
There is treasure in our dreaming
From the soul to the eye,
For whenever we gather in the light of God's grace
and for all who we remember
There will even be a place.

IN THE QUIET

There is a Place

There is an old story found in Irish tradition concerning an old man and a young boy who went walking one day into the fields. Taking some rest, the old man lay down and fell asleep. As he slept, the young boy saw a beautiful butterfly emerge from the old man's mouth and fly off towards an ancient ruin at the end of the field. After a short while, the butterfly returned and re-entered the old man's mouth. He awoke and told the young boy that he had fallen into a deep sleep and had a dream. In the dream he found himself in an ancient ruin and found there some hidden treasure. The young boy and the old man set off immediately to the ruin, and there they found the hidden treasure.

In the folklore of Ireland, the butterfly is often associated with the 'soul', which can leave the body when a person sleeps. Following on from this was the belief that the souls of the dead can also move freely about. Because of the nearness of the 'other world', it was not a fearful thing to pass into the next life. It is the place of eternal summer, of everlasting youth – Tír na nÓg. It is the place without fear, pain or sorrow, but above all it is the place of friends and neighbours. So passing from this world to the next is like a homecoming, expressed indeed by many poets and writers in the Irish tradition down through the years.

In the contemporary world, there is a desire to avoid the pain of death. The quest to sustain life for as long as possible, the desensitising of grief and the avoidance of speaking about death isolates us even more when we experience death within our own circle. There was much to be said for the old Irish custom of wakes, when life stopped and people made time to 'celebrate' the life of the one who had passed away Such customs and traditions allowed family and friends to grieve in an open and natural way. Surrounded by friends, relatives and neighbours, those who mourned were assured of support and sympathy. Suppression or camouflaging our sense of loss can only lead to further sadness, expressed in many kinds of ways as modern life has shown us.

Though we cannot see and touch those whom we love and miss, we are very close to them. They are aware of all we do, as from their place of eternity and wisdom they are not limited by time and space. I love the old belief that souls were so small that two of them could converse while doing their purgatory at either side of a leaf. Just as the souls of the dead were very close, so too was Heaven – as a Kerry woman once said, 'Heaven is a foot and a half above us' – or 'only a breath away'.

Those who are in Heaven, in eternal light, guide us towards the way of God. For with God there is no distance, no barrier and no death. One of the most beautiful texts that I have come across is a prayer poem from the Isle of Aran, off the west coast of Scotland. In this prayer, which is a litany of prayers around the theme of death, the poet prays for *bás gan bhás* – death without death. It is a beautiful prayer

Death with oil
Death with light
Death with hope
Death without fear
Death without hate
Death without death.

The notion that family, friends and neighbours would gather in waiting for the soul that has passed on is an image that is so natural for the Irish spirit – where *muintearas* – community and belonging – are so intertwined with Irish life. So remembering the dead is an integral part of daily living. To ignore or dismiss such tradition does grave injustice to the memories of departed souls.

Two friends of mine decided to return home from the United States to be married in the west of Ireland. It was to be an Irish and Scottish wedding, a gathering of the Clans, with the bards and the musicians. The couple had requested that I compose a piece of music for the event and were very conscious of the absence of both their 'fathers' who had departed this life.

How does one write a piece of music for a wedding and yet include a theme remembering those who had passed on?

I based my composition on one of the central beliefs of our faith – 'the communion of saints'. Each time we gather in the presence of the Lord for Eucharist, our Heavenly family joins with us – and why wouldn't they? The song reminds us that when we gather to celebrate our faith in God we are never alone, as our Heavenly family joins with us, but it also reminds 'them' of our constant and eternal love.

On the night before the wedding the aged mother of the groom – who had been unable to travel due to illness, passed away. It made the song even more poignant and yet there was a sense of rejoicing that beyond the limits of time and space she could now celebrate with the Heavenly Family at an even greater banquet.

In writing under the heading of 'Songs of Tears', I was aware that certain songs pertained to particular events that bought sadness and sorrow. It is out of such events that often great beauty is born, as we know only too well from our history in terms of music, poetry and literature. However, on the 14th of September 2001, I was asked to sing 'There Is A Place' at a special Ecumenical Service for those who had perished three days previously in the terrorist attacks in New York, Washington and Pennsylvania. Like many people, as a regular visitor to the United States, it was difficult to believe that over three thousand people had died due to an act that defies understanding.

As I stood on the steps of the altar of the Pro-Cathedral in Dublin to sing, I remember gazing down at the faces – the President, the members of the Irish Government, the Diplomatic Corps, the American Ambassador and his wife and other such dignitaries. I saw not politicians and officials but rather the human face of sorrow, the human face of vulnerability, the human face of God. Many tears were wept that week, in sorrow, in loss, in disbelief. Loss is great when love is great. But such love does not end in death. The death and resurrection of Jesus Christ is a reminder of this. In our Eucharistic prayer we are constantly reminded of the 'communion of saints', i.e. our loved ones, our friends and neighbours, the saints and all who belong to our heavenly family united with us in prayer.

The ancient Celts believed that the *Dealan-Dé* – the Golden butterfly – was a soul on its way to Heaven. Perhaps they got it right, that in the most fragile and most vulnerable of lives lies great and rare beauty., but is only a foretaste of the beauty that awaits us.

In the quiet of the evening at the close of the day
We will rest on our journey to the Lord we shall pray.
May we thank God for blessings, for the moments we've shared
As we seek for tomorrow, close by us you'll stay.

THE LORD WILL HEAL THE BROKEN HEART
The Lord will heal the broken heart
God will seek the lost and find him.

SACRED STORY

The Lord Will Heal The Broken Heart

One of my greatest regrets in life is that I was very young when my grandparents died. The Japanese have an ancient saying, 'Happy the home where liveth three generations', that I fully agree with, as the wisdom of age is a great blessing, and I have no doubt that grandparents who enjoy the presence of their grandchildren are kept young at heart. Now with less commitments they can afford to enjoy time with their children's children.

My grandmother Anne, from Cork, had a great love of music, and the oral tradition that she respected brought her to many weddings and funeral parties to share her gift. Inviting her to sing at such occasions was both an acknowledgement of her gift but also a witness to the important place of music in the life and ritual of Irish life. In the tradition singing was an integral part of community occasions and the music maker beheld a place of high esteem.

I have always been a great believer in the 'healing' qualities of music and it is borne out in studies of many cultures. However, in our own Irish culture the ancient tradition of 'keening' was most important. The keening song, or *caoineadh* as it was known, was the lament sung at the death of a great hero, a friend, a neighbour, or loved one. Women who were known for their ability to keen and lament were invited to mourn the dead and in most cases needed very little encouragement. Some of the laments were mere words which were specific to the person in question while others were actual keening songs, some of which have survived through the years. Many of these songs identified with Mary, the Mother of Jesus – a grieving mother who suffered much. Such songs were influenced by the medieval music of the twelfth century that eventually found its way into Irish culture. A common example in Ireland is the song 'Caoineadh na dtrí Mhuire' (The Keening of the Three Marys). There were specific words used in these songs. One such word is *ochón*, difficult to translate into English and yet with powerful onomatopoeic resonance, conveying a sense of loss, pain and grief.

In the ancient days of the Celts the greatest form of music was the song known as the *aidbsí*. The word *aidbsí*, in its simple, ordinary signification, means nothing more than 'great' or 'greatness', but in its technical musical significance, it means the singing of a multitude in chorus. The word *aidbsí* would appear to have been used also to denote the lamentation at great funerals where one man or woman sang the praises of the dead to a specially appropriate air and at the end of each verse a murmuring chorus joined in. Its sound, it is said, though produced in the throat, was not unmusical or monotonous but one capable of various modifications of distinct, musical tones ascending from the deepest bass to the highest treble. Such singing at the end of each verse was known as *ag crónán*.

I am sure you have often heard the phrase about an old woman 'crooning' in the corner – by this it is meant that she is humming to herself some kind of tune. In fact in its purest anglicised form the word 'old crone' derives from this ancient Irish tradition – *ag cronán*. This tradition of lamenting or praising was also found in Scotland but was called *cepóg*, although this term is not used today. Such music, I believe, allows the communal expression of grief and sadness or praise and jubilation. The singer becomes the vehicle by which the community can express their feelings and believe that the chosen singer is the adequate response to a given situation.

I am always touched by a story told to me by a Franciscan priest who had the sad and difficult job of telling an Irish Travelling family that their little boy had just died in a city hospital. Saying nothing, the mother left the caravan and went into a nearby field where she sat down and began to keen. Her cries of lament would touch any heart as she cried aloud, 'Why, oh why have you taken the one I loved?'

One of my sad disappointments in ministry is the lack of participation by Irish Catholics in the music of liturgy. I cannot help feeling that we miss out on so much by leaving the business of worship and music to a specific group, i.e. the choir and musicians – after all 'that's their job', or so rests the belief. Very often when I sing at a particular liturgy I am faced by a sea of faces, some listening attentively, some who may be bored but also by some who would love to sing but haven't the means to. Devoid of texts and music we wonder why people don't sing. Some people, however, have a greater understanding of the place of music in worship. It is no coincidence, as someone once wrote, that the 'voice is placed between the head and the heart', between the place of intellect and emotion. The human voice is the means of communication for us, be it the voice of hope or the voice of despair, the voice of encouragement or the voice of discouragement. In the Indian tradition of Sanskrit, the place of singing is greatly respected. The phrase 'nada brahma' is used to express the divinity of music and singing so powerfully. *Brahma* means the creator, God, the underlying principle of the whole universe. *Nada* means sound. Directly translated the phrase means 'divine sound' or 'divine singing'. We often hear people saying 'he or she has a divine voice', an acceptance of a beautiful gift well used.

The song 'The Lord Will Heal The Broken Heart', from the collection *Sacred Story*, is a song of hope, and though I have often heard it sang on many sad occasions, it tells us that in the midst of our trials and difficulties God *does* listen and healing will come, though perhaps in a way or time when we do not expect. The melody of the piece is recognisably Irish and was written out of a tradition that despite much suffering, never lost hope. There is an old Irish saying, *Is giorra cabhair Dé na an doras* – God's help is nearer than the door. There has always been a belief in Irish spirituality that when Christ is present, hope is not lost.

I believe that the songs of people like my grandmother, sung into sacred spaces, do not end there, as prayer does not end but re-echoes through time and space to call another generation to keep singing. Hopefully my song will continue her song, and many more will come to join me in the tune.

> I will bless the Lord all of my days
> I will bless the Lord and give God praise
> For the Lord will heal the righteous soul
> May the peace of God by your life and hope.

AFTER THE RAIN
After the rain
I will see the earth washed clean
Flowing from the Sacred streams
Flowing though, the parching land
After the rain,
I will see the face of tears
Turn to joy and sing of peace
Love will come
After the rain, after the rain.

IN THE QUIET

After The Rain

In 1999 I was invited by the Siamsa na nGael Committee in Chicago to audition as a soloist for the premier of Shaun Davey's work *The Pilgrim Suite*. There are a number of traditional Irish songs in the work and it was felt that my style of singing would suit. Having been offered the part, I launched myself into learning the music, working alongside Frank McCourt, author of *Angela's Ashes*, who was the narrator of the script and a gentleman to work with.

This is a beautiful composition based on the travels of the early Celts and combines the various musical traditions of Ireland, Scotland, Wales, Galicia and Brittany. Each piece is a wealth of history, opening a window into pilgrim travellers of bygone days. Some of the early Celtic saints such as Columcille feature in the work as well as such characters as King Arthur.

It is a unique combination of musical instruments – classical and traditional – with special emphasis on the art of piping, combining the Scottish bagpipes and the Galician *gaitas* (pipes) and the Irish uilleann pipes.

For me, one of the most beautiful compositions in the work is the piece entitled 'The Deer's Cry'. The lyrics are taken from the Irish scholar Kuno

Meyer's translation of an eighth-century poem, sometimes, but apparently incorrectly, attributed to St Patrick and usually entitled 'St Patrick's Breastplate'. This prayer poem served as a prayer for protection against the dangers faced by medieval travellers and contains the lines:

> I arise today
> Through the strength of Heaven
> Radiance of moon
> Splendour of fire
> Speed of lightning
> Swiftness of wind
> Depth of the sea
> Stability of earth
> Firmness of rock.

In these lines, the reverence of the early Irish writer for the Creator and His creation is very much in keeping with a spirituality that embraces the universe – the cosmos. The natural surroundings were the sanctuary of the Divine. The trees were the Cathedrals that pointed to the majesty of the Creator. God was reached, touched and worshipped in the wild beauty of the landscape. The rising sun brought the promise of tomorrow. It wasn't difficult for the first Irish Christians to embrace the culture of a people who already reverenced the earth they belonged to – a sacred hiding place of God.

So too did the early Irish monks see in such a landscape the mark of God the Creator who offered mystery, colour, music, beauty and healing. The dream of God for His people was reflected in their spirituality and though born in remote holy places, was carried to the four distant corners of the world.

The cultural landscape of today is vastly changed and many people have lost the will to dream or to retain a sense of sacred awareness. In a world that has experienced much growth and development, we are slow to acknowledge the ecological bereavement that is taking place, for every two thirds of a second a child dies from hunger, and forty million people die of a hunger or hunger related diseases each year. Seventeen thousand species have become extinct and the ozone layer continues to be depleted. Such situations can cause predictable results where oppression, violence, discrimination become the norm. Unfortunately very often the 'religion' and the spirituality associated with particular groups have not helped – as they have not been at the service of transformation and change. Where are the voices of church and religious leaders when sanctions continue to be imposed on the most vulnerable and poorest of people? Very often the religion of such regimes will support rather than confront.

The composition 'After The Rain' was inspired after I was invited to participate in a conference entitled Courage at the Crossroads. It drew together people from many nations who were examining the challenge of environmental issues from a Christian perspective and who were influenced by the vision of people like Edmund Rice, people who fed the hungry, clothed the naked and brought hope to those who were paralysed by despair and imprisoned by poverty.

As I sat and listened to the various speakers, I realised that I knew little about the world that was placed in my care – the gift of God to this humanity. I was so busy in my own 'little' world, I no longer had a dream for tomorrow that included others.

What happens when we have the courage to dream – when we share a common vision? We can begin to believe that tomorrow can be different, that we can overcome despair and resignation, that we can believe, as Brian Swimme wrote in *The Universe Story*, that 'To dream is to summon the psychic energy and moral courage necessary to move into the future with responsibility and hope'.

In the Divine imagination, great beauty was born and offered to us for our care. Instead we have abused, wasted, ignored and pillaged the gift. I believe it is not too late to dream again. Mother earth has the ability to heal herself if we could take the time to consider such implications and what they mean for us.

There is a sacred rhythm to the earth that must be respected. People die not because there is a shortage of food, but because we waste so much. Tomorrow can be different if we want it to be. This is what dreaming is about. Perhaps as the song suggests, we need to take time to reflect on the beauty of the Divine imagination that offers us this sacred earth but expects us to nurture and protect also. We need to see the stars again and clear our vision of limitless junk and imprisoning pollution.

The early Irish writer of 'The Deer's Cry' understood the sacredness of the earth, its wild untamed beauty, the hiding place of God. As never before we have choices to make. What kind of world are we willing to offer to the generations yet unborn? Perhaps in answering this question we might take courage in the simple yet eloquent words of a little four year old child from Russia:

May there always be sunlight
May there always be trees
May there always be Mama and Papa
May there always be me.

Suantraí

—❦—

Songs of Dreams

THE MAIDEN AND HER CHILD
In a bitter December
On a night cold and still
In a cave by the moonlight saw God's plan fulfilled
A cry fills the night sky
Oh, where does heaven hide?
While the world is sleeping silently
The maiden lulls her child

ANCIENT WAYS, FUTURE DAYS

The Maiden and her Child

When I was commissioned by Veritas Publications in Ireland to edit a new national hymnal in 1999, I had a great desire to include as much Irish music as possible and within this, as wide a variety as possible, spanning many years and if I could, centuries. There was, however, one genre of music that I longed to be able to include in the collection. It was a collection of the oldest Christmas carols written in Ireland over four hundred years ago. I had heard some of these pieces sung by the great Irish singer Noirín Ní Riain with the Monks of Glenstal, but the carols themselves had their origin in the small sea fishing villages off the south east coast of Ireland in the county of Wexford.

Within this county lies a great history – a story of risings and revolution, of danger and despair, of hope and freedom, and of a people who refused to let the ancient traditions die. About 150 years after the Reformation, a man called Luke Wadding, the Bishop of Ferns (Wexford), published a collection called *Pius Garland*, which contained ten Christmas carols, some of which are still sung today in the small fishing village of Kilmore in Wexford. That was in the year 1684. It is believed that the music of these carols had their origin in the folk tunes sung by the people of the area and by using such music it was thought that it might enrich the liturgy. These were difficult days for church and state and yet old traditions die hard. The carols were protected and their singing continued. Some years afterwards new life was given to the tradition in the birth of William Devreaux in 1696.

Devreaux's family had lost their lands due to the Cromwellian campaign and had settled in Wexford. In 1724 he went to Spain to study theology and returned four years later in bad health. During a period of convalescence in his father's house, it is said that he wrote several Christmas carols. In 1730, when he was strong enough to begin work again, he took up parochial work in a small rural area, with no church except the 'corner of a field' where the faithful would gather for Mass. He died in 1771 at the age of seventy-five. Since then tradition has it that the Devreaux name has always carried on the tradition of singing of these carols – right up to the present day.

Devreaux's collection was called *A New Garland*, following on to Luke Wadding's *Pius Garland*. The carols have survived with a number of families in the area as 'protectors' of individual carols. They continue to be sung over the Christmas period in this area of Kilmore. There has always been a certain amount of secrecy and care of the carols. Tradition seems to indicate that the choir consisted of six men who divided themselves into two groups of three to sing the alternate stanzas. The carols are sung unaccompanied in free tempo with the emphasis on the individual style of the singers. As Christmas approaches, the carol singers gather in one of the local houses to maintain the tradition. Such customs rely on the goodwill and commitment of the families involved. It would be a great pity to see the tradition die.

It is fascinating to think that such a tradition was born into an Ireland when its people knew great suffering and deprivation and yet they have been loyally protected down through the years by the various families within this small area off the south east coast. The 'Enniscorthy Carol', sometimes known as the 'Wexford Carol', is one that is most commonly known from this area, though written at a later date and some times mistaken as one of the Kilmore carols.

When I was writing the text of the carol 'The Maiden and her Child', I wanted to use an old traditional Irish melody to make a connection with the past. The melody I chose is in traditional Gaelic style and was commonly used for an advent hymn called 'O Comfort My People'.

To sing such music builds bridges with the past and makes sacred connections. Much of our traditional music was born in hearts that knew much suffering, who found their freedom in songs and melodies lifted up to God, far beyond borders and boundaries, which may have imprisoned the human body, but *not* the human spirit. When I was teaching at Knockbeg College, Carlow, I taught some of these carols to the pupils, and in a culture of rave music, rap and rock, I was enthralled at how these young fellows took to singing the carols and how proudly they performed them. Knowing that they were the 'keepers' of an age old tradition became almost a sacred duty for them.

Christmas in Ireland holds many customs rooted in the early Gaelic culture that have survived the ravages of time and modernity. Though simple in form, they retain a spirituality that has still much to offer to a noisy, post-Christian world. Perhaps it is time to rediscover our sacred and ancient symbols.

For centuries it has been the practice to leave a lighted candle in the window of the house. This flickering light was a symbol of welcome to the Holy Family who sought shelter as on the first Christmas Eve. The ceremony of lighting the candle was one of the simple ancient rituals during which prayers were said for departed loved ones. The privilege of lighting the candle was usually given to the youngest child in the house. The candle also served as a signal in times past to any priest seeking shelter and protection – a sign that he was welcome in this house and that it was safe to celebrate Mass there.

The lighting of candles can be traced back to antiquity, to the time when the ancient Romans lit their candles at the midwinter festival to signify the return of the sun's light after the winter solstice.

The lit candle throws light into all kinds of corners, and with a breath of wind the flame dances and casts its shadows suddenly on unsuspecting subjects. It may show up the dust but it also offers a way in the darkness. In reviving such traditions we offer to others the light of welcome. Perhaps we are a nation that will forever be haunted by the old Irish prayer, 'Often, often comes Christ in a stranger's guise, Often, often, see Christ in the strangers eyes', as sadly nowadays, the light of hospitality is dimmed to the *new* strangers who pass our *darkened* windows and *bolted* doors.

The music of today that screams out to us in early October from neon shopping malls are a far cry from the corner of a wet wintry field in Kilmore where the carols were first sung, and yet the message hasn't changed, nor has the need to still find some room at the 'Inn' for the new poor and homeless. If we are to honour the singing of our ancient carols perhaps it is time to re-light the candle in the window and open once again the door to the Irish hearth.

Across the many centuries
Across the days and years
May God's shadow fall upon us
May we know the Child of peace
For the same star is shining
To our lives now drawing nigh
In each heart a voice is calling
'Tis the Maiden and her Child.

CANTICLE
Great and wonderful are your deeds
O Lord God, the Almighty
Just and true are your ways
Oh, King of ages.

THE CLOUDS' VEIL

Canticle

It is not uncommon as you drive through many Irish towns and villages to
see the ruins of early monastic settlements dotting the skyline. Such ruins
hold great secrets and are encrusted with melodies and memories of other days.
Once the wellsprings of great faith, it is now so easy to drive by and become
immune to their very presence.

The town that I grew up in was a small midland town called Edenderry at
the edge of the boglands of Allen. Its name derives from two Irish words –
Éadan Doire – meaning 'the brow of the oak'. It was a woodland area with a
monastic settlement dating back to the early thirteenth century. Since then
there has been an abundance of ecclesiastical and military ruins in its vicinity.
I find it difficult to imagine that from the Norman invasion in 1169 to the end
of the Tudor Conquest of 1603 it was the scene of continuous warfare, with
each campaign leaving its mark on castle and monastery.

The present town owes much of its design and origin to the plantations of
the eighteenth century and in particular the Marquis of Downshire (1753-
1801), who oversaw the development. Influenced by the Georgian era of
architecture, there are still a number of historical buildings to be seen. Today it
is a thriving town in the hinterland of Dublin where many commuters find
peace and tranquillity away from the chaos of city life.

As far as I can remember there has always been a great tradition of music in
this town, and as a young boy I had many opportunities to explore the world
of performance. I owe much to those who gave of their time and talent to

provide such opportunities for the community to gather together and celebrate. These were the people who helped us to laugh when times were tough. I am sure there have been characters in every town and village in our country that taught us how to laugh at ourselves and kept us from taking ourselves too seriously. Such are the people who inspire and bring wonder into a young boy's imagination, which would eventually fire him to harness the talents and energies that may otherwise have remained dormant. I owe them much.

I also remember, as a young boy, my first experience of sacred music. There had always been a tradition of good church music at St Mary's, my local church, and proudly I can say that such a tradition continues today.

It was here that I first experienced the sound of Gregorian Chant. The now deceased parish priest, Monsignor Martin Brennan, insisted on having a 'High Mass' each Sunday which included all the rituals befitting such a celebration. We might have been a small country town in the heart of Ireland but Rome itself would have been envious of our liturgies, even though the much loved curate, Fr Jack, was not renowned for his abilities as a fine tenor!

There was always a sense of solemnity about this Mass and though those days have been consigned to memory, they are still very much alive in the senses. Every time I smell incense I am transported back to other days. It seems that such music was never far from my memory. Today, no matter where I am, when I hear the Missa de Angelus I become a young boy again, almost touching the 'smells and the bells'.

What was it about this music that has struck a chord so deep within my psyche? Perhaps it has something to do with its unmeasured or 'free' rhythm – the melodies do not have the regular 'beat' that is characteristic of much of the music of the early church. Was it that this 'free rhythm' gave the music its spiritual quality as the soul sang its way towards heaven? Whatever it was, I do know that it was this sense of liberation that appealed to me very much and still does.

Some years later I entered the seminary at St Patrick's College, Maynooth, known throughout the world as the training ground for Irish priests both at home and abroad for over 200 hundred years. While there I joined the seminary choir and became immersed in the Gregorian tradition. Now I was given an opportunity to understand the meaning and development of Gregorian Chant – the music I had heard so often as a young boy – the Sacred Music of the Church. I discovered how this music was used for the singing of the Divine Office (The Prayer of the Church) and for the liturgical celebrations, and how it developed due to the vision of Pope Gregory (590-604), who founded the first singing school, known as Schola Cantorum, in

Rome, to train singers for the church. He also organised the church's annual cycle of liturgical readings and first established the church's authority over the secular rulers of Rome. So how was this music discovered?

There are a number of stories and legends associated with Gregory. There are paintings depicting a bird singing chants into his ear as he wrote them down – unfortunately there was no suitable musical notation at that time! There are also stories of his sending out missionaries with instructions to bring back any new music they encountered, with his famous saying, 'Why should the devil have all the good songs'. With such a long and established history, it was fitting that such music would be sung in the beautiful Gunn Chapel at the Maynooth College, the largest stalled church in the world, as Sunday after Sunday we would gather to sing the praises of God.

However, as my views of music began to change, or as I began to broaden my musical canvas, there were times when as a young seminarian in a contemporary world I rebelled within. I found it very difficult to have to constantly turn to the *past* for repertoire, to sing for the people of the *present*, who were trying to find a way to bring the Gospel message into the *future*. Perhaps there will always be that tension between past and present, which is both healthy and life giving. I believe that we must strive to maintain a proper balance, to hold what was good from the past but also to ensure that the creative forces are encouraged and supported. And yet I do believe that it is difficult to find music to match the eloquence yet simple beauty of a Gregorian Kyrie or some such piece.

During the past year, as I studied for my M.A. at the University of Limerick, I often sought the peace and tranquillity of the Benedictine Abbey of Glenstal at Murroe, near the south-west coast of Ireland. The Abbey, which is dedicated to saints Jerome and Columba, is home to a community of monks who live the rule of St Benedict. The monks manage a boarding school for boys, a farm and a guest-house, and assemble in church five times a day for the Divine Office and the Liturgy of the Eucharist. Set on a 500 acre estate with woodland, steams, lakes and gardens, it is a place of calm.

Through my visits to Glenstal, I began again to revisit my childhood memories of chant and ritual song. The ancient books called it 'the song of the angels', as it stills the soul for union with God. The sacred singing of the chant is very important in Glenstal and the monks have made many recordings themselves. They have also recorded with Irish singer Noirín Ní Riain, a unique and beautiful voice that I have had the pleasure of working with on a number of occasions.

When it came to writing the piece 'Canticle', its inspiration and influence was without doubt the ancient Gregorian tradition. Based on a psalm from the

Book of Revelation, I used a contemporary sound with male voices and a female soloist. This is the piece of music that I use as the opening sequence to many of my concerts. Simple yet haunting, it is an invitation to pray, to still the heart and enter into a sacred place. In the ancient tradition, *lucenarium* was the term given to the lighting of the evening light for prayer and in concert we always light our candles during the singing of this piece to highlight the sacred time and place we experience together.

These days, when I travel to far off places, I find great consolation in hearing such music, especially if I am tired or weary and need resuscitation. Each time I hear the singing of sacred chant my mind finds a quiet corner of its own and wanders back through the corridors of time to my days as a young boy, listening to the sweet notes of the Credo as they floated high above the high steeple of St Mary's, to join with the universal praises of God. After all, as St Gregory once said, why should the devil have all the good music!

Who shall not fear and glorify your name
For you alone are Holy
You alone are Holy.

ALLELÚ – MY GHRASA MO DHIA

Allelú, Allelú, Allelú mo shlaínitheoir,

'stú mo Dhia

'smé do ghiolla

Allelú, mo chroí go deo.

SACRED STORY

Allelú – Mo Ghrasa Mo Dhia

I am often asked the question, 'What inspires you?' or 'Where do the ideas for your next piece come from?' Not always easy questions to answer, but I believe that once we open our mind to a creative process we begin to be more perceptive of things that otherwise might go unnoticed. For example, when I started writing texts for my compositions, I began to read more and more poetry. I once heard an author say that 'poets are frustrated musicians'; there are many times in my own situation when I would say the reverse is also true!

The creative process is unending and I am always fascinated by the various connections that can take place within this process. While I was composing the music about the life and times of Edmund Rice – the founder of the Christian Brothers – I came across the name of a man that Edmund Rice had befriended. Tadhg Ó Súilleabháin (Timothy O'Sullivan) was born in County Limerick in the small village of Turnafolla in 1715. Known to be well educated, he spent his time as a travelling scholar staying in the homes of the people and educating their children. He was a classics scholar in Greek, Latin and Hebrew. At that time Ireland was in the throes of the Penal Laws which forbade the education of Catholics and the practice of their religion.

Wandering poets and scholars like Tadhg Gaelach were vital in keeping the spirit of people alive, using their poetry as a means of preserving the national spirit – there was always the promise that all would be well when the Stuarts regained the throne in old England.

In his early years, Ó Súilleabháin gained a reputation for his political views, often ensuring the anger of clergy and politicians, but fate was about to change the life of Tadhg Gaelach. It is said that under the influence of a saintly Bishop Richard Walsh of Cork, and the friendship of Edmund Rice, Tadhg Gaelach's life was transformed and illuminated. Records show that Ó Súilleabháin often met with Edmund Rice in an ale house called The Yellow House Inn, where he was well known for his singing. The influence of such people on his life was very telling, for within a short space of time it is said that he abandoned the writing of poetry about current affairs and instead dedicated himself to the writing of sacred scripts and songs. He wrote for a collection called *Pius Miscellany*, which includes some of the most beautiful prayer-poems ever found in the Irish tradition.

He continued to travel from house to house using the opportunity to write and teach. He would often be seen on a Sunday evening praying in the Cathedral of Waterford City. His fervent wish was, *'Bás naofa, in áit naofa, lá naofa'* – a holy death, in a holy place on a holy day. Soon, however, his wish would be fulfilled, as on the Sunday after Easter Sunday in 1795, having received Holy Communion, he died on the steps of the Cathedral. He was buried in a borrowed grave in Ballylaneen, Waterford, in a family plot, owned by friends who had often offered him lodgings and rest. On a spring day in April 1795, another great poet and friend, Donnacha Rua Mac Conmara, then eighty years of age, bade Tadhg Gaelach an eloquent farewell.

In the collection *Sacred Story* I set the text of one of Tadhg Gaelach's pieces, 'Mo Ghrasa Mo Dhia' (My Love, My God), to music and added a refrain to the piece. It has become one of my favourite pieces to perform and one that I also set in the English language in the collection *Ancient Ways – Future Days*.

In the winter of 2000, while studying at the University of Limerick, I received a telephone call one evening from Oslo, Norway. The caller had discovered that the music of 'Allelú – My Ghrasa Mo Dhia' was in fact not three hundred years old but rather three years old and that the composer was not some nameless author from the past but someone who was not very much older than himself! He was requesting permission to record the piece. I was rather surprised that an Irish language sacred song might be suitable in Scandinavia, but I was soon to be proven wrong. The piece arranged by Sean Kjartan was recorded by Norwegian group State – a young male singing group who specialise in close harmony singing. The song went straight into the charts at number 9 and climbed all the way to number 5 at Christmas of 2000. It became a hit for the group through a series of highly successful concerts with the famous Harlem Gospel Singers from New York on a European tour.

When I hear this song I am presented with many images, contemporary and ancient, with sounds that are mystical, evocative and yet numinous. It is difficult to imagine the connection between an old poet wandering from house to house seeking shelter from the harsh winter and the young agile singers full of life and vitality who enthral thousands with their moving harmonies and infectious enthusiasm, both singing from the same text though centuries and minds apart. I believe that in the Divine Imagination such connections are never coincidence but rather are part of the dream of God for all of us, where time and space are not a concern.

Perhaps the dreams of Tadhg Gaelach Ó Súilleabháin were conditioned by his time and place in life, but his prayer goes forth, continuing to inspire and heal, and has allowed countless others the chance to dream.

Ever more I'll sing your praise
Ever more through endless days
God of all seasons, right and reason
Lord of love and endless grace.

COULD IT BE
So fly the soul, to its secret abode
Seeking some word to lighten the load,
Could it be, could it be
that God would right the wrong
Could it be, could it be
that God would hear my song.

LIGHT THE FIRE

Could It Be?

It was a place of hustle and bustle, streets thronged with shoppers and revellers. It was over thirty years ago and I remember it vividly as if it was yesterday. It was the week before Christmas and my parents, my brother and I joined the madness of the Christmas rush to find the last minute bargains as if there was no tomorrow.

It was early in the afternoon when 'it' happened. I became separated from my family and began to search frantically for them. Walking through the door of a department store I became swamped in a huge sea of people and became completely lost. I ended up walking from Henry Street to Moore Street in the heart of the city of Dublin. I was terrified and sobbed uncontrollably. Eventually I was found by a kindly woman, a street trader, who tried desperately to console and reassure me. There are many things that pass through one's mind in such times and to this day I can still recall the thoughts of panic and fear that overtake you. The woman who had found me had by now summoned half of Dublin as a search party and I distinctly remember her giving orders to a group of skinheads. They looked like they were taking orders from an army commander as they set about looking for my parents with great immediacy. How they were going to find them was beyond me, as to this day I still don't believe they ever knew who or what my parents looked like. It was all part of the great adventure.

Meanwhile my frantic parents were also searching. As I stood at the corner of the street, with by now a swollen red face, holding a huge balloon given to me by the woman who found me, I saw my parents telescoping the crowds. Standing alongside them was my brother dressed exactly like myself, both of us in similar green coats – my twin. It would have been easy for the police to identify him, but in the mind of a frightened six-year-old such things belong to the adult world, I never thought of telling this fact to the police. And, as if it were yesterday, I remember the terror, fear and panic evaporating as I was enfolded in the secure and loving arms of my mother. The prodigal son had been found and he hadn't even got a chance to squander anything, as he was too young! Eyeing the huge balloon, my brother wondered if he got lost could he get one too? No such luck as we were firmly in the grip of two frightened but loving parents.

To this day, whenever I walk the same streets, I can sense the anxiety of those moments, but also cannot forget the kindly soul who stepped out of nowhere and became an angel for an afternoon – and of course not forgetting her troupe of emissaries.

Ever since I can remember I was a twin. My brother was always there. We played, prayed, fought and sang, were always together right up until the day I left home to go to college. Such closeness comes with a price. Separation is not easy and yet there is a natural yearning in all of us to be free, independent and have our own unique story heard. Many people today are denied such basic fundamentals of human rights – to live free and independent lives. Having an identical twin is like always knowing there is another side of the argument. It's like always knowing that at least someone will tell it to you as it is, and yet there is something innately comforting about this.

The freedom to go our separate ways, to make different life choices, to accept the weaknesses and strengths of one another is all part of the journey of life that only such siblings can know.

Of course, being so alike, there have been many incidents of mistaken identity with my twin, particularly when people jump quickly to the wrong conclusions and think that I have been secretly supporting a wife and four children somewhere!

Having enjoyed such companionship since the moment of my conception, I have always struggled with being alone, and yet this struggle has been at the very heart of my creative journey. I have always needed solitude to listen to the inner voices that inspire the creative process. From the solitude comes the inspiration, the images and the song, though it is not always easy to find this place of belonging. The great poet and Spanish mystic, St John of the Cross, struggled with this and writes beautifully and movingly. He distinguishes between *loneliness* and *solitude* – one is destructive and dark, the other is life-giving and fulfilling. Such a journey from loneliness to solitude is never easy and yet experience teaches us that great beauty is born from great pain. The author John O'Donoghue uses a beautiful phrase from the west of Ireland – *Is farach an áit a gheobfá gliomach* – it is in the unexpected or neglected place that you will find the lobster.

Solitude does not call us to live as isolated individuals caught up in our own little world, but rather to take time away so that we can then truly appreciate the giftedness of ourselves and that of others. In solitude I discovered the courage to begin to write and compose – to shape and reshape words and notes into new creations and forms.

To bring one's work out into the light is a fearful process. As with any artist, your work is that part of your innermost thoughts and aspirations that is difficult to expose, but with each step there comes new courage. I can still remember the fear of presenting my first composition in public and all the negative thoughts that run with it, but I also remember the encouragement of other voices. This is what carries us towards the next unveiling. Such voices of assurance will in time drown out the voices of self-doubt that can so often afflict us in the most sacred moments of our creative process

There are a number of places that I have always found conducive to solitude, places of quiet beauty that inspire me. There is one particular place whose lake is so beautifully imprinted in my mind that I find myself wandering there at all hours in time, in the secret garden of the heart. Such places are a gift of solitude.

Other times I like to meet with friends where the angst of my own life is quietened by the reassurance of loving support. Such people are like what the old Celtic prayer called a 'necklace of light' in our lives, enriching us and lighting the darkness that can often surround us.

In my place of solitude the song 'Could It Be?' was born – born from my struggle to find my true identity – a journey from dependence to independence, from fear to freedom, from isolation to inspiration. It is a song that I love to sing, as in doing so I realise the many blessings that have been poured upon my life.

It is a song that we all sing at least once in our lifetime though dressed in a different melody or a different lyric. It is a song about Divine longing, the deepest and most ancient of needs in all of us. It is where I am most vulnerable and where I am most blessed. It is where I communicate with my God. There is a great hunger in our world to find such solitude. To journey from a place of isolation to the place of knowing, the place of healing.

Rather than finish this page with my own text I have chosen some lines from the dissident Iranian poet Ahmad (1926-2000), who in his exile wrote:

at night,
when the silver moonstream
makes a lake of limitless plain
I spread the sails of my thoughts
in the path of the wind.

Such lines remind me of my secret garden where hopefully I will return, when the day is done.

Seol

Seol, seol, seol
Seol sa bhealach suan
Seol, seol, seol
Seol I'm chroí go buan.

Follow Your Heart

Seol

On a September day in 1998, as I sat in a restaurant of a well-known Dublin hotel with two colleagues from a record company, little did I realise what was about to unfold. They asked me to write a song in the Irish language for the European Song Contest known as *Eurosong*, which gives exposure to performers and writers and has been associated with such names as Cliff Richard, Abba, Celine Dion, and, of course, *Riverdance*.

I accepted the challenge on condition that I could choose the performers and arrangements myself. It is difficult to find a space for ethnic music in a contemporary culture yet I believe there is a depth in our traditional language that will never be matched by the 'tele-text lingo' of today.

I sat down and penned the song 'Seol' (pronounced *shole*). Meaning 'Sail', it is a lullaby to soothe the soul. I loved the musical quality of the word *seol* – the sense of calm that it evoked. So with the song complete I was ready to record the demo. I approached the internationally acclaimed trio, The Vards, who I had already had the privilege of working with on a hugely successful album entitled *Heavenly*, and they agreed to sing the song with Cathy as lead vocalist. My brothers Tom and Gay and myself were the backing vocalists. With a combination of three sisters and three brothers the natural harmonies worked very well.

With hundreds of songs received and nearly all of them in the English language I wasn't over-optimistic, though I had every faith in my performers. After a lengthy process the song was eventually chosen as one of the eight finalists. So began the story of 'Seol' and a journey that I wasn't exactly ready for!

The pop star Ronan Keating, who had just split from international pop group Boyzone, also had a song chosen for the competition, so the tabloids had a field day. 'Priest and Popstar do battle' ran one newspaper front page. Suddenly I found myself in the middle of a scenario that I wasn't prepared for. Rather than judging me on my musical merit, I began to be questioned about all kinds of religious and personal issues. I began to receive anonymous letters, including some that requested I not sell my soul to the devil. Some groups began praying that I would lose the contest, lest I be 'lost' forever. The British TV channel Channel Four ran a story comparing me with Fr Ted – a sit-com that had little or no comparison with my own life (or so I sincerely hope!). Slowly but surely I began to understand the 'power of the media' and the many different interpretations of *truth*.

John Drummond had done a beautiful arrangement with the Concert Orchestra for the song and a number of people had begun to place the song in the top three. Some bookies ran a book on me and though I was tempted I didn't have a flutter!

A documentary on my life and music was aired on television the week before and this enthused the media even more. It was both a challenging and a difficult time for me, for though I enjoyed working at such a professional level with the musicians, singers and production teams, I also felt quite isolated. I was aware that no other priest or religious had travelled this journey before. To some I was a hero, to some a freak, to others a lost soul, and to myself just someone who was expressing a gift but just in a different way. I have always struggled with lack of funding and resources in the world of liturgical and sacred music and have on occasions been tempted to put my energies into secular music, but something has always called me back. Perhaps its where I am most rooted, and yet I know I have much to learn from those whose life blood is found in the highly competitive world of commercial music and all that flows from it. Perhaps such tensions will always exist in the world I inhabit, caught as if it were between two worlds.

Back in the real world we continued our rehearsals. Three sisters and three brothers is not exactly a recipe for organisation but there were great times that taught me how to laugh at myself again. On the night of the song contest final, Cathy, Wendy, Lisa, Tom, Gay and myself took the stage to sing our composition 'Seol', televised to over one million viewers. The bookies had now placed us as favourites and I knew that Louis Walsh, the great impresario who was managing Ronan Keating, was anxious. I also knew that a number of people were on their knees praying for the 'protection of my soul'. I was destined to lose one way or another.

As the voting began to take place the studio was very tense, but win or lose I was happy I had achieved what I had set out to do, i.e. to write an Irish language song in a contemporary setting.

In the final outcome as the votes poured in, we were pipped at the post by an outsider and took second place. I was disappointed for the others and I had already been booked for a radio show the next morning, perhaps in anticipation of my winning, but I still went ahead and took part. I am quite certain there were parties in some quarters however! Within a few months I had been approached by Sony Music to write some new material for Cathy Vard's solo album, including the title track 'Follow Your Heart'. I was very proud of the final outcome. I have continued to work with The Vards and we have become great friends.

Travelling between two worlds allows one to see the fickle and the fantastic, the shallow and the deeper sides of life. In both worlds I have much to learn and indeed one world can learn much from the other. The world of the stars, the world of images and arts can teach us much, as can the world of the sacred where the values and dignity of each person is accepted for who they are, and not what they have achieved.

I have learned that there is a much greater depth to people far beyond the idle gossip of tabloids or the reckless judgements of gossip columns. The real winner in the end is not the _sensational_ but rather the _sincere_.

Travelling between two worlds has allowed me to see the best and the worst of both worlds. We can not close our eyes to life around us and the price of progress, but if we go empty hearted into the future without tending to our spirits, we do ourselves and those who come after us a great disfavour.

Not long ago I had the honour of singing at the funeral of the great Irish actor and storyteller, Eamon Kelly. A true master of his art, he was able to recreate scenes beyond our wildest imagination in the small corner of a stage and enthral young and old with his stories of heroes and myths and the ordinary things of everyday life that we often miss because we are in such a hurry. He was blessed with a great wit and was never short for a word. He was a legend of stage and storytelling but never lost contact with his roots, or his faith story. He was comfortable in both worlds, in the world of the sacred and the world of the secular, and not embarrassed in either. I am sure he would enjoy my closing lines...

Not long after my Eurosong contest debut, I was at a party one night where I was approached by a young lady whose attire was more suited to the set of a Mad Max movie (i.e. spiked hair and black make up). She told me she had seen me on the television and then said, 'I was really disappointed for you.' I was rather surprised that she would even be remotely interested in this genre of music. But she continued, 'Yes I really hoped you would win. In fact I kept praying the Memorare (a prayer to Our Lady) during the voting!' I was totally taken aback and my faith in human nature was definitely restored. Sometimes doors are open into new worlds when we least expect it and I have no doubt that such connections are all part of the Divine plan for all of us.

Seol ar t-aoide oír, 's mé i dtaoibh go deo
Sail on a golden tide , and I forever by your side

IN THE QUIET
Be still O be still,
For I am your God
Be still now and listen
And you will hear my word
Be still, O be still
Deep within your life
For you will find me —
In the Quiet.

IN THE QUIET

In The Quiet

The story is told that a wise old hermit who lived at the edge of the woods came home one evening to find his hut being burgled. Standing at the doorway, he watched as the thief searched through the meagre belongings of the old man. The thief turns around and is startled by the presence of the old hermit who tells him, 'Take what I have – here is my rice bowl and here is my sleeping mat and my tunic, but there is one thing I have that you will never possess'. Curiosity got the better of the thief and he asked, 'And what is that?' The old hermit took him by the arm and led him to the edge of a small pond. 'This is what you shall never take from me,' said the old man as he pointed to a beautiful silver disc floating on the surface of the water – the reflection of the silver moon, which illumined the night sky. 'This is one thing that you can never take from me.'

I am always moved by this story, not only because of the beauty of its imagery but because of the challenge to look closer at the world with the 'inner eye', to see the things that usually pass beyond us because we don't have time to see them.

I am constantly asked when and where I write my songs, and I usually respond by saying that I can only write when I go into an undisturbed space –

for me that's usually between 11.00 p.m. and 2.00 a.m., and not always easy to find. If I am working to a deadline it demands time and discipline, neither of which come easily to me. When I am composing I do value 'the quiet' and it is one of the few times when there is no noise, no music playing, nothing but the stillness.

From earliest times, people have withdrawn to find the quiet place, to reflect, to heal or tend the soul. Whether it be a philosopher's cave, a holy mountain or a lonely lakeside, people are drawn to seek solace and silence. Today we are no different.

We all know of places that offer shelter to the searching soul and if only we could stay in the stillness for long enough we might begin to notice the very different sounds that surround us, followed by the abundance and diversity of colour. Slowly but surely we may even hear the music that comes from the silence of our own hearts.

There are some places that nurture and heal my creative imagination and cause me to hear new songs, but sometimes I am slow to withdraw to the 'quiet place' as it is in this place that I 'meet myself', as a Kerry woman once said, 'I take myself aside and have a good chat with myself'. The silence is like a mirror, as it reflects back to us the shadows and pain that write lines of worry on our faces. But the silence can also remind us of the hope and opportunities offered to us constantly which we fail to see in an otherwise busy world.

The song 'In The Quiet', also the title for my latest collection, was born out of my need to visit the place of silence, for often the voices of the world become so loud. In the midst of travelling, post-graduate studies, composing and writing, and pastoral duties, it is easy to fill the day with business and miss the beauty of the 'moon reflected on the water'. It is much easier to be the 'bride at every wedding, or the corpse at every wake', or the centre of everyone else's life except your own, than to take the time to explore the silent music of life. There are boundless melodies in such silence, but you need a special wavelength to tune in. We are told that God speaks in the silence. I have discovered that my longing to write and my longing to sing is an expression of my longing for God. Such longing is nurtured in the silence.

Music is my bridge to reach the Divine. It takes me into another world, where I long to bring others also. The healing power of music can never be overestimated and when music is wedded to prayer it goes beyond us and echoes throughout eternity. When I finish writing a piece of music I like to think that it will find value in the dream or plan of God. In returning the creation to God, I can no longer be possessive about the gift. In the hands of God, it can do infinitely more than I will ever do. This has been proven to me many times, in ways I could never imagine.

A young couple who lost their little child once told me that they played a piece of mine constantly for three months as it helped to heal their loss. Another lady I know asked that the music accompany her in her final illness as it removed all fear of parting from her life. Such stories I tell not of boasting but in gratitude that out of silence, and struggle, something good is born.

As I write these final words it is in the early hours of the morning, the twilight zone, I am surrounded by the silence, alone and yet the moment is full of sacred memories of another full day. Nearby, the Sisters of St Clare continue their all night adoration in prayer – a consoling thought that in the silence of the night the voice of prayer is heard, rising far above the sleeping community nearby...

When souls are hurting and they don't know why
When hearts are broken and children have to cry
When prayers are spoken late into the night
You will find your answer if you come into the quiet.

ON THE JOURNEY
On the journey, seek the light of the day
On the journey, heaven blessing we pray
On the journey may God's fortune descend
We seek the Lord of the Way.

THE CLOUDS' VEIL

On The Journey

*T*he first pages of this collection began in the quiet and rustic townsland of Kilcredan, situated in the unspoilt beauty of east Cork, off the south coast of Ireland. It is there that I return as I conclude my reflections.

When I was a young boy, my family made a yearly trip down to Kilcredan for our summer holidays. Eagerly awaited, the holiday began with the long journey through the centre of the country, arriving in the late evening to much excitement and welcome. As we neared our destination, it was the custom to count all the white washed walls until we stopped at the one that was to be our home for the next few weeks. There was also another tradition that I still hold dear to this day. On arrival, we would climb the stairs of the farmhouse to look out from a particular window that opened up a panoramic vista of the surrounding countryside – our first glimpse of the sea. For people like ourselves who were land-locked for eleven and a half months of the year, this was a sacred moment – a glimpse of another world.

In the distance, nestling in the foothills, was Ballycotton Bay – a picturesque fishing village lying twenty-five miles south-east of Cork City. A mile from the shore is Ballycotton Island, with its famous lighthouse built in 1851. This village has provided shelter for many a ship and sailor down through the centuries. The lighthouse has guided many a wandering ship to safety in the midst of the dense mist and fog that often descends like an eerie veil.

My abiding memories as children are twofold – the reflection of the light shimmering like a jewel across the water's surface, or the silence of the night broken by the sad sound of the fog horn calling out to ships that passed in the night.

Such images often come to mind when I am worried or anxious, when I feel like a ship without a sail, drifting into deep waters or surrounded by a dense mist – when the creative muse abandons me and I worry where the next note or lyric will come from. In these times there have always been beacons of light, people who blow the wind back into my sails when in the midst of stormy waters and who guide me safely back to the shore.

I talk not only of fellow performers and artists but of ordinary folk who continue to travel with me on this journey. I have shared moments with people whose stories will never be known on earth, but I am certain are written in the book of Heaven. Such people have had a profound effect on my life and work. In ancient Ireland the wandering musicians, the bards, sought refuge and support among the chiefs and clans of the time. Such support enabled the bard to express the inner longing that called him to create. Many artists and musicians I know have shaped the stories and songs that come from my page, though they may not know it. Whether I am working in small rural communities, in recording studios or in broadcasts, or working with worshipping communities, there is always something to be learned and always someone who can inspire the creative process to begin all over again.

As I look back on my journey so far, I am constantly reminded of the goodness of humankind and especially of the contribution of people whose days on this earth are now over. That the poets and pipers of generations past can still inspire us today is a great tribute to their craft, but sadly, often the wisdom of past days can soon be forgotten in the name of progress.

My songs would still lie in the bottom of a chest somewhere, were it not for the foresight and courage of people who saw a place for such music. I will forever be indebted to the people who helped me in the early days of my career. It has always been my passion to sing and to call others to do the same; for when I sing I lose myself in the memory of other days, or in the dream of a new tomorrow. There is a time when the songs of joy, songs of tears and songs of dreams need to be heard in our lives. There is a desire in all of us to sing, to express who we are, where we have come from, and what we would like to be. Why else would the Divine imagination of God create such a gift without expecting it to be used.

Recently I gave a lift to a young refugee from Nigeria. We spoke of his country, his tradition and his people. He was a percussionist and in the course of our conversation I asked him if he liked to sing. I was both taken aback and somewhat saddened by his response, 'What have I to sing about?', a sentiment that might be widely expressed by many today.

Yet I firmly believe that our song can become our expression of freedom, our hope of belonging, our chance to heal the wounded places of our lives. The haunted longing of many can be fulfilled when they are invited to belong and to sing their song. Each voice may have a different song, a different sound, but blended together can become a universe of beauty, an orchestra drawn together by the Divine conductor.

The freedom songs of Africa, the sean-nós or traditional songs of Ireland, the Gospel songs of America, and the Chant of Eastern monks, all reflect the beauty of the Divine songwriter. To be a small part of this is a gracious honour, but far greater is the privilege to be able to call others to join, so that their song, too, is heard.

Where will my next melody come from? Who will inspire my next lyrics? I am not sure, but of this I am certain, that they will be sculptured and shaped by the experience of ordinary people who constantly remind me of the beauty and diversity of the Divine imagination of God.

As I write these last words it is autumn now. Outside my window the berry trees are laden and the once green lawn is now a moist carpet of rustic reds and browns. In the ancient times this was the time of rest. When the harvest was gathered and the long nights had reclaimed their place it was a time for recalling and reflection. A time when neighbours would gather to recall the stories of the past year, sing the songs of other days and dream dreams as they prayed into the future. Such moments were the lifeblood of the community, telling the story and offering belonging. Late into the night the kitchen floor became the universal stage and the heroes, hunters, and hounds of past epics were recalled in the wild imagination of the storyteller. The dancers took to the floor in the midst of cheering onlookers as the Kerry polkas were heard echoing through an open window, carried on the wind. Such were the days when time was suspended and songs sung were carried to the far corners of the world, remembering absent friends and those who had been called to their eternal homeland. Such were the songs of my grandparents and my grandaunt – songs that have shaped our world and made us who we are today. In their memory and in the memory of all, I pray God that I can continue to sing, for many years to come, the song of my people.